IN
THE
NAME OF
SUBMISSION

IN THE NAME OF SUBMISSION

A PAINFUL LOOK AT WIFE BATTERING

KAY MARSHALL STROM

MULTNOMAH · PRESS

Portland, Oregon 97266

Scripture quotations, unless otherwise indicated, are from the Holy Bible, New International Version, © 1973, 1978, 1984 by the International Bible Society. Used by permission of Zondervan Bible Publishers.

Scripture quotations marked NASB are from the New American Standard Bible, © The Lockman Foundation 1960, 1962, 1963, 1968, 1971, 1972, 1973, 1975, 1977. Used by permission.

Cover design by Al Mendenhall and Dave Haidle
Edited by Liz Heaney

IN THE NAME OF SUBMISSION
© 1986 by Kay Marshall Strom
Published by Multnomah Press
Portland, Oregon 97266

Multnomah Press is a ministry of Multnomah School of the Bible.

Printed in the United States of America

Library of Congress Cataloging-in-Publication Data

Strom, Kay Marshall, 1943-
   In the name of submission.

Bibliography: p.
   1. Abused wives—United States.   2. Abused wives—Services for—United States.   3. Abused wives—United States—Religious life.   I. Title.
HV6626.S77   1986   362.8'3   86-18217
ISBN 0-88070-163-3 (pbk.)

86   87   88   89   90   91   92   93   –   8   7   6   5   4   3   2   1

FOR THE
ABUSED WOMAN

You are an important and worthwhile person.

You deserve to be safe from fear and injury, especially in you own home.

You deserve to be treated with respect.

You are not to blame for being beaten and abused. You are not the cause of your husband's violent behavior.

No one has the right to accuse you of liking or wanting the abuse.

You do not have to take it.

If you believe your staying will help your husband, you are wrong. Your leaving may be the very thing that shocks him into realizing his behavior is against the laws of man, and more importantly, against the laws of God.

You do have responsibility for your own life. With God's help you can make changes if you really want to.

You are not alone. God is with you.

If no one knows what is happening, there is nothing anyone can do. Stop hiding. Talk to someone. Ask for help. Others are ready and willing to help you.

God is all powerful. There is no problem he cannot solve.

God has promised to be with his children always. Trust him!

CONTENTS

TO THE READER

We live in a violent society. To see proof of this one need only turn on the television set or open the evening newspaper or read the current movie reviews. For many people even home, instead of being a safe haven, is a place of pain and fear and anger and frustration. For some it is a place of death.

Wife abuse is by no means the only form of domestic violence. Wives also abuse their husbands, parents abuse their children, young people abuse their parents, adults abuse the elderly. There are even different levels of wife abuse. It doesn't always result in black eyes and broken bones. Deep wounds are also caused by emotional abuse, humiliation, and verbal harassment. While not minimizing the damage inflicted by such abuse, this book deals only with the repeated, nonaccidental, physical violence of a man against his wife.

In the Name of Submission revolves around the story of Janet, a battered woman. Let me tell you a little about Janet. First of all, she is not me. This is not a personal experience account. In fact Janet is not any one person—she is a compilation of several women. Every battered woman's story is unique. In the telling of any one, there are sure to be aspects that will not be generally applicable to most readers. There will also be important points that do not apply to the woman whose story is being told, but which must be considered by others. In order to include all of the subjects I considered important—the children, the role of the church, the question of submission, the importance of dealing with the husband—I chose to combine the stories of several women.

Until a few years ago I knew almost nothing about battered women and abusive men. I had no idea of the prevalence of this occurrence, and could hardly believe it happened in Christian homes. The problem of wife abuse was first brought to my attention by my good friend Judi Bumstead. A Licensed Family Counselor who has herself worked with battered women within a Christian context, Judi told me of her concerns about the need for awareness and action on the part of the Christian community. I am deeply indebted to Judi for her help, guidance, and encouragement throughout this project.

Perhaps you picked up this book because of your concern over an abused friend or relative. Good for you. You are already taking the first step toward helping her.

It may be that you yourself are a victim. I am glad to see that you are moving toward taking responsibility for your life.

Or maybe you just want to become better informed about a problem you see so much in the news today. You are to be congratulated on being concerned enough to make yourself aware.

Whatever your reason, this book is for you. For it is only when the abuse is understood and faced by those involved, by the Christian community, and by society as a whole that the problem can be stopped and the victims healed. Once there is awareness, many good people, many Christian people, will be ready and willing to listen, to understand, and to help. Pray with me toward this end.

Kay Marshall Strom
Santa Barbara, California

1

JANET'S
STORY

A s soon as Janet saw Roger at the door, she knew what was coming. Fortunately the children had already had their dinner, so she hurriedly sent them upstairs to watch television and then get themselves to bed.

"Be careful," Janet told herself. "Everything has to be just right. Stay calm and don't do anything to upset him."

Roger growled about having had a terrible day at work. Janet nodded sympathetically, but she was careful not to speak. Past experience warned her that anything she said might be the wrong thing.

Glancing around the living room, Roger spotted a stack of magazines Janet had intended to take out to the trash. "This place is a pigpen! Don't you ever clean up? What do you do around the house all day anyway?"

Janet mumbled an apology and rushed over to get rid of the magazines.

"I'm starved!" Roger growled. "What's for dinner?"

Janet caught her breath. *This is it*, she thought. *He's not going to like dinner, and I'm going to get it.*

"I asked you, what's for dinner?"

Panic welled up inside her. Struggling to keep her voice even and controlled, she answered, "I made meatloaf and mashed potatoes—lots of mashed potatoes. I know how much you like them. And there's apple pie for dessert. It will be on the table in a minute."

To her great relief, Roger said nothing. Maybe she had been wrong. Maybe this wasn't going to be one of those nights. Maybe, just maybe, things were going to be different this time. And so she let down her guard.

When Roger saw the dinner table, his eyes flashed and his jaw stiffened. "Why did you have to use the tablecloth your mother made? You know I don't like it!" He grabbed the table-cloth and jerked it off the table, sending plates, utensils, glasses, and platters of food crashing to the floor.

Terror seized Janet. *This is it,* she thought frantically. *I've got to get out of the house. I've got to get away.* But the children were upstairs; she couldn't just leave them. Unsure of what to do, she hesitated. And then it was too late.

Grabbing her by her hair, Roger threw her to the floor. He hit her again and again. He called her horrible names. He tried to choke her. Janet begged him to stop, but her pleas only made him angrier. The last thing she remembered was her head slamming against the floor.

When Janet woke up, she was lying on the sofa. Roger was standing over her. "I'm sorry, Honey," he said. "I'm sorry I had to do it. Why do you have to make me so angry? Why can't you do things the way I ask you to? If you would just obey, I wouldn't have to punish you like this."

Janet never wanted it to be this way. She hated yelling and fighting and anger. There had been enough of that when she was a child. Ever since she could remember her mother and father had bickered and argued and fought, sometimes so badly that she and her sister and brother were convinced their parents would kill each other.

Her parents were hard on their children, too. It wasn't so bad for Janet because she was quiet and cooperative, always determined to do anything necessary to keep the peace. But her brother and sister couldn't take what they considered the injustice of their parents. They were always pushing to the very limits. And they paid dearly for being "headstrong," "troublesome," "bad" children.

Janet and Roger first met in college. Although he was four years older than she, they were in the same class. "He is so mature!" she had bubbled over the telephone to her sister, Lenore. "He was in the navy for four years, so he's much older than the other boys around here. And he is so interesting! He's been everywhere and he's done everything. Not only is he handsome, he's smart, too, and a good athlete, and thoughtful and considerate."

"Nothing like Dad," Lenore had commented dryly.

Janet's Story

As a matter of fact, Roger *was* the opposite of Janet's father. Perhaps that's what made him so attractive to her. While her father was loud and boisterous and bossy, Roger was quiet and sincere and considerate. Janet's family had never been religious—especially her father, who insisted that any man who couldn't run his own life didn't deserve to be called a man. It was different in Roger's family. They called themselves Christians and were all active in their church. Patiently, and with feeling, Roger had told Janet about his own personal relationship with Jesus Christ.

"Christian men are good and kind and loving," Janet told Lenore. "Christian men aren't like our father."

"He sounds like the catch of a lifetime," Lenore said with a laugh. "I think you should marry that man!"

And that is exactly what Janet did. Actually, she would have preferred to wait until they graduated, but Roger was insistent. He was ready to settle down. "Besides," he pointed out, "You don't need a college education. One wage-earner in the family is enough. I want my wife to stay home with the children where she belongs."

The first year of married life was wonderful. Janet persuaded Roger to let her work at the switchboard in the administration building of the college while he finished school. She enjoyed her job and loved being a part of college life. And she was so proud of her new husband! Not only did he get academic honors, but athletic awards were heaped on him as well.

Not that their marriage was perfect. But then, what marriage is? For instance, it soon became evident that Roger had a much quicker temper than Janet had expected. At times she was at a loss to understand what she had done to set him off. When he was angry he said cruel, insulting things to her. One time, when she tried to defend herself from his insults, he slapped her face. After that she kept her mouth shut and tried to remember that he talked that way only because he was angry. He didn't really mean it.

Then came the day Janet went off to work and unintentionally left the front door of their apartment unlocked. Taking advantage of the open door, someone came in and robbed them of their new color television set, a camera, and a radio. Janet was upset and angry with herself, but Roger was livid. He screamed and yelled at her and called her "stupid," "fool," and "idiot."

"If you're going to act like a child, I'll have to treat you like a child!" he yelled. "You will have to be punished!"

Roger's punishment loosened two of Janet's teeth and blackened her eyes. She was horrified at his violence. But, she reasoned, she had deserved it.

"I'm sorry," she told Roger through her tears. "From now on I'll be more careful, I promise."

Janet thought this would be the end of the problem, but she was wrong. It was just the beginning.

2

WHAT
KIND OF MAN
WOULD DO
SUCH A THING?

B efore she was even awake, Janet was aware of the throbbing ache in her head. When she tried to turn over, a sharp pain seared through her left side. She opened her eyes to a grey and cloudy day.

"Good morning," Roger said cheerily. "I've brought you coffee and orange juice. Your omelet will be ready in a minute."

"My side hurts," Janet mumbled in confusion. "And my head . . ." Several minutes passed before she remembered the reason for her throbbing head and painful side.

"What you need is a nice, lazy day in bed," said Roger as he fluffed up her pillow. "The kids are already up and eating breakfast, and I've made arrangements for them to spend the day at my mother's house. Now what I want you to do is eat a good breakfast and spend the day reading and watching old movies on television. I'll be home at noon to check on you and bring you something special for lunch."

After a quick kiss on the cheek, Roger hurried downstairs to check on the omelet. Janet, watching him go, was suddenly struck by how little he had changed in their twelve years of marriage. He was still the same tall, tanned, good-looking guy she had fallen for so many years ago.

He really is a good man. In spite of everything, he really is a good man. How many other husbands would take charge like this? I mean, breakfast in bed, the kids arranged for, a whole day to myself . . .

And yet, there was last night and her bruised and swollen face. She cringed as she remembered Roger's rage as he pounded her with his fists and kicked her again and again. And all because she used that tablecloth.

Who is Roger, anyway? Is he the monster of last night or the loving, concerned husband of this morning? Trying to figure it out made Janet's head ache more than ever.

No Such Thing as an Abusive Type

One of the most perplexing elements of the battering syndrome is this very matter with which Janet is struggling. Roger is a confusing combination of violence and gentleness, cruelty and love. What is it that causes a seemingly normal, caring husband to turn into a batterer? What kind of men are batterers?

Everyone has inadequacies. All husbands, like their wives, sometimes lose their tempers. But not every husband grabs his wife by the hair, pulls her to the ground, and kicks her in the face.

Some professionals say that wife beaters are basically bullies who give in to their irrational flashes of violent rage. Others disagree. They claim that the pressure of many things going wrong in the men's lives trigger their attacks. Still others insist that wife batterers are simply men who suffer such deep emotional pain that they cannot deal with the stresses of life.

On one point the experts do agree: The crux of the problem is that somehow abusive men have learned to deal with their anger and frustration through violence.

The problem of wife abuse is complicated by the myths surrounding the issue. On the few occasions that Janet did tentatively reach out to tell someone what was happening, her attempts were always met with the same response: "Roger? Oh, come on! He's not the abusive type!" And each time she heard it she wanted to scream out, "What do you know about 'the abusive type?'" But she never did. It was much easier and far less embarrassing to simply change the subject.

When a man does not fit the stereotype of a wife abuser, people find it hard to believe that the battering is really going on. How could such a nice guy be capable of beating and battering his wife? What Janet's friends don't understand is that there is no such thing as "the abusive type." This denial by friends and associates only reinforces the batterer's belief that his actions are right in the eyes of God and man. Consequently, he sees no reason to change.

COMMON MYTHS ABOUT WIFE BATTERERS

Here are some of the most common myths about wife beaters, followed by the facts. You may be surprised!

What Kind of Man Would Do Such a Thing?

Myth 1: *Wife battering is a problem of lower-class families.*

Fact: Batterers are found in all levels of society and cut across all economic, racial, ethnic, religious, and geographic lines. They can be doctors or lawyers or college professors. They can be mechanics or plumbers or politicians. They can be rich or poor, educated or illiterate. Every segment of our society is affected.

Myth 2: *Batterers are losers—financially, socially, and emotionally.*

Fact: Like Roger, many wife beaters are successful, churchgoing, well-liked, nice guys. They are often charming and pleasant to others; many are highly respected in their communities. People outside their home frequently see them as good providers, warm and loving fathers, caring husbands and law-abiding citizens. Only their families see the violent side of these abusive men.

Myth 3: *Wife beaters are sick, psychotic men.*

Fact: Certainly some are, but counselors tell us that by far the majority lead normal lives in every way except that they are unable to control their aggression. Although many batterers do seem to have two personalities, unlike true psychopaths they usually feel a deep sense of guilt—and shame—for what they have done.

Myth 4: *A man would not do such things if his wife didn't deserve it.*

Fact: Many, many people believe this myth, including many battering husbands and abused wives. "I wouldn't hit my wife without a reason," insisted Jim who had just broken his wife's arm. "What do you think I am, an animal?"

Yet it has often been noticed that no matter how a batterer rationalizes his actions, his beatings are rarely warranted by the actual events that triggered them. Susan, Jim's wife, was beaten for breaking the yolk while frying his egg one morning. Rachel's husband exploded in anger because their little son got the first piece of his birthday cake instead of his father. Justine was beaten because she fixed frozen dinners for supper. How could such trivial incidents ever justify the beatings, broken bones, and blackened eyes that followed them? Those who still are not convinced should talk to Helen. She was sleeping when the beating started that put her in the hospital for three days.

Many psychologists now believe a batterer's rage actually has little to do with his wife—or with anyone else for that matter. They say it comes from within himself.

Myth 5: *Because they have usually been drinking, battering men can't control their violent behavior.*

Fact: Drunkenness, like mental illness, is one of society's conventional explanations of wife beating. A 1978 Gallup Poll found that almost one in four persons interviewed believed that alcohol was the cause of family trouble.[1] But the professionals are not convinced. While it is true that many batterers were drinking just before an attack, many experts maintain that abusive men use their drunken condition as a convenient excuse for their violent behavior. Certainly alcohol lowers a person's control and inhibitions against violent behavior, but it does not necessarily follow that alcohol causes the tendencies toward violence.

Alcohol may be the trigger that lets loose a man's pent-up rage and violence. Then again it may merely be a cover-up for violence that was going to happen anyway. "I didn't know what I was doing—I was drunk" is an often-used and often-accepted excuse.

Myth 6: *Wife abuse does not affect Christian families. Christian men do not act this way.*

Fact: Wife abuse does occur in Christian homes. One need only look at the recent rash of articles on the subject, and the stories they relate, to prove this. After a special section on wife battering appeared in the December 1983 issue of *Family Life Today*, the editor stated, "The relevance of this topic to our readership was emphasized by the record number of letters sent to us from Christian women who are or have been victims of wife abuse . . . more than we have ever received in response to any article in the magazine."

What Kind of Man Would Do Such a Thing?

CHARACTERISTICS COMMON TO BATTERERS

While there is no such thing as a typical abuser, there are characteristics that are common to many abusive men.

The majority were raised in abusive homes. Over half of all abusive men were either themselves abused as children or else witnessed their fathers abusing their mothers. Less than one-quarter had what could be called good relationships with their parents.[2] Domestic violence has a nasty way of reproducing itself generation after generation after generation.

Most are unable to communicate effectively. Battering husbands tend to find it very hard to understand and express emotions other than anger. Anxiety, fear, frustration, affection—all of these end up being expressed the same way. Their physical violence is not usually an expression of anger toward their partners, but rather more likely a ventilation of their own feelings of inadequacy and frustration. Many experts feel the violence of wife beaters is the result of pent-up frustration and anger that has been repressed.

Most batterers believe in sex-role stereotypes. Many are overly concerned with living up to a tough, self-sufficient, masculine role. They believe a husband should be in charge, his every word unquestioned law. Many were raised to regard women as childlike or as possessions. They believe their position as man of the house gives them the right to direct and control their wives and, when necessary, to punish them and to force compliance.

Often rigid and uncompromising, abusive men really believe that wives should be punished for violating their husbands' rules. And good wives, they reason, should be content to be controlled. Over and over police hear the same astonished, indignant response from abusive husbands: "You mean I can't beat my own wife?"

The majority have a deep need to hide their weaknesses and insecurities. Many, many batterers suffer from crippling insecurity, immaturity, and self-doubt. By being physically dominating, they try to reassure themselves that they really are strong and in control. Because they feel weak and powerless, they resort to violence as a way to prove their power and masculinity.

24

Although they go to extremes to present a "macho" image, batterers are highly dependent on their wives. That's why a batterer is particularly dangerous when his wife threatens or tries to leave home. Beating her is his one chance to be the oppressor instead of the oppressed. Through physical force these men seem to gain the sense of power they are unable to feel anywhere but home. It is not hard to understand why husbands who are unemployed or dissatisfied with their jobs are more likely than others to abuse their wives.[3] Because they lack a sense of control over their own lives, they determine to at least control their wives.

Batterers often fear losing their wives. Because he so desperately fears losing his wife, the batterer often tries to make her stay close to him by being possessive and jealous. He may even attempt to isolate her from her friends and family. Afraid that she will become friendly with someone, he may refuse to allow her to get a job. He may go so far as to check her car mileage and time her errands. If she's late, or if her mileage doesn't check out, he is convinced she is seeing another man—so he beats her.

Batterers commonly accuse their wives of unfaithfulness; they voice great fear of being abandoned or "cheated on." Because free access to money gives a woman some degree of freedom, many abusers maintain complete control over the family's finances. When other methods of exerting control fail, they may resort to threats, either to kill their wives or to kill themselves. And these are not always empty threats!

Their wives are a convenient scapegoat. The wife beater has no idea who he is really trying to hurt. Although it's small comfort to his injured wife, she likely is not the one he really wants to destroy. The real target may be his parents, or perhaps his business associates, or even himself. So why does he strike out at his wife? Because she is the most accessible target and she has little chance of escaping or getting back at him. Furthermore, he knows that society is not likely to interfere.

They often blame their abusive behavior on their wives. It is next to impossible to get an abusive man to admit he has a problem. Like Roger, they often blame their wives for their violent outbursts, even though the woman may have done nothing more

25

than choose the wrong tablecloth. After a beating some batterers regularly demand, "Why did you make me do it?" In the opinion of abusive men, it is their wives who are responsible for any and all of the problems in their relationships, so they deserve whatever they get.

For most there are times of remorse. "You needed to be punished," Roger had patiently explained to his sobbing, bleeding wife after this last beating. After picking her up off the floor and laying her on the bed he had gently wiped the blood from her face and the tears from her blackened eyes. Then he had kissed her tenderly. "I'm sorry I hurt you so badly, Janet," he continued, "but you did need to be punished. You can see that can't you?"

It's not unusual for the batterer, when he sees the truth of what he has done, to become frightened and to try to make up to his wife. But even while apologizing and pleading for forgiveness, few batterers can accept the responsibility for what has happened.

There are men who, although they fit many of these characteristics, never show any signs of violence toward their wives. There are also successful husbands who don't drink, were raised in healthy families, show signs of good self-esteem, and demonstrate no jealousy, who nevertheless beat up their wives. *It is important to understand that the characteristics mentioned here only put a man at risk of becoming a batterer.* But being at risk is not the same as being destined to act in a specific manner. Whatever contributing factors and tendencies exist, in the end the responsibility falls upon each person to decide his or her own actions.

CHANGE IS DIFFICULT

The majority of abusive men have no interest in changing because they don't believe that what they are doing is wrong. If a battering man meets no formidable resistance, either from his wife, church, friends, or from the authorities, he becomes so comfortable with his lifestyle that it easily becomes a pattern.

When an abusive man discovers he can get away with hitting his wife, he hits her more and more. Eventually, as her emotional health declines and she becomes less and less able to cope, her abuser loses all respect for her. As he becomes more experienced in battering, he becomes more aggressive, and as he becomes more aggressive, the potential for serious injury and death rises.

What about abusive men who go into counseling? Do they change? It depends. Because batterers tend to either deny or minimize their violent actions, they seldom seek treatment on their own. If they maintain a defensive position, insisting that their behavior is justified, improvement is unlikely. As long as he continues to see violence as a comfortable and successful way of resolving his conflict and releasing tension, he sees no reason to change.

Most abusers drop out of treatment after only a few sessions. This isn't surprising. Being confronted by his problems and the results of his actions makes him increasingly anxious and uncomfortable.

Yet there are those who do stick with the therapy, and for them the outlook is quite good. There are those who have succeeded in stopping their violent behavior. Some men, having come to understand their own behavior, no longer look to their wives for somewhere to place the blame. They have learned to look to themselves.

Brian is one batterer who finally won out over his violent behavior. What caused him to stop for good? Here's how he explains it: "My counselor asked me how I'd feel if my little girl married someone like me when she grew up. I told him I'd kill any monster who laid a hand on my daughter! Then all of a sudden what I had said hit me. That monster I was threatening to kill was me!"

Life can be frustrating and disappointing for all of us. There are times when it is downright miserable. At such times it can feel very good to lash out, to punish someone for our pain. But most of us do not respond to the stresses of life with violence. We understand that self-control is part of being civilized.

Before he can change, a battering man must realize that what he is doing is wrong. It is imperative that his actions not be excused or

27

minimized—not by his wife, not by his friends and relatives, not by the church, and not by the authorities. Wife beating is against the law. A Christian who is also a batterer must come to see that God hates his violence. He has no right—in the eyes of God or man—to beat his wife.

Yet even the most determined abusive men find it almost impossible to stop the violence alone. After acknowledging that they have a problem beyond their control, they must be willing to go for help. Part of getting that needed help is being willing to go through some embarrassing and painful personal disclosures. It's extremely hard to continue in therapy when tender areas are touched and long-hidden wounds exposed. The need to rationalize, to make excuses, and to shift the blame can be overpowering.

"I didn't think I was that bad," Brian now confesses. "In spite of what I did to my wife, I thought of myself as a pretty nice guy. As it turned out, I was more mean than nice!"

Perhaps it's precisely because so many batterers are "nice guys" that they are allowed to persist so long in their terrible, destructive behavior. Even when their actions come to light, relatives, friends, neighbors, authorities—even their own wives—cannot believe that the men were capable of such actions. And so excuses are made and the violence goes on.

> If only there were evil people somewhere
> insidiously committing evil deeds,
> and it were necessary only to separate them
> from the rest of us and destroy them.
> But the line dividing good and evil
> cuts through the heart of every human being.
> And who is willing to destroy a piece
> of his own heart?
> —Aleksandr Solzhenitsyn

1. Richard J. Gelles, *The Violent Home: A Study of Aggression between Husbands and Wives* (Beverly Hills, California: SAGE Publications, 1974).

2. "Black and Blue Marriages," *Human Behavior Magazine* (June 1976).

3. One of the first to touch on this subject: John E. O'Brien, "Violence in Divorce-Prone Families," *Journal of Marriage and Family* (November 1971, vol.33, no.4).

3

WHAT KIND OF WIFE WOULD ALLOW IT?

The ringing doorbell jarred Janet from her sleep. Startled and confused, she sat upright. But the now familiar, sharp pain ripped through her side, and she fell back onto her bed.

Again the doorbell rang. "It must be Roger," Janet thought. "He said he would come home and check on me. I guess he forgot his keys."

Gingerly, Janet dragged her aching body out of bed, put on her bathrobe and stepped into her slippers. She felt weak and dizzy. After only a few steps the pain in her side forced her to stop. Gasping for breath she reached out and steadied herself against the wall. The doorbell rang again.

When Janet finally got the door opened, she was surprised and embarrassed to find that it wasn't Roger at all. It was her sister Lenore.

"Jan!" Lenore gasped. "What on earth happened to you?"

It suddenly occurred to Janet that she had not yet looked in a mirror this morning. Was it possible she looked as bad as she felt? If only she had put on some makeup. If only she had not answered the door.

"You poor thing!" Lenore exclaimed. "Were you in an accident?"

"Yes," Janet answered quickly. "I was in an accident. I slipped and fell in the bathroom."

Pushing past her sister, Lenore entered the house and closed the door behind her. Taking Janet's arm she led her to the sofa. Then she pulled over a chair for herself and sat down. "Tell me about the accident," she said.

"Well, I don't know . . ." Janet stammered. "There really isn't much to tell. I was cleaning the bathroom and I guess I slipped and fell. I must have hit my head on the sink or something. I don't remember that much about it."

Lenore looked at her suspiciously. "Come on, Jan," she said. "What *really* happened?"

Janet stared down at her hands, clasped tightly in her lap. She said nothing.

"It was Roger, wasn't it?"

Janet tried to protest, but her voice cracked and her eyes filled with tears. She was so confused, so frightened, so angry, so embarrassed.

"I can't believe Roger would do this to you!" Lenore exclaimed. "Janet, why do you stay with him?"

THE BATTERED WIFE SYNDROME

If women wouldn't stay and endure their husband's violence, wife abuse would not exist. But Janet does stay, and she is not alone. Some women put up with incredible abuse, and still they stay year after year after year.

The wife of the late Eisaku Sato, former prime minister of Japan and recipient of the 1974 Nobel Peace Prize, said she stayed even though her husband beat her regularly once a week.[1]

Sara stays even though her husband beat her with a broomstick and poured boiling water on her just before reminding her, "You'd better get ready, Honey, or we'll be late for church."

Brenda stays even though her husband broke her arm while she was recuperating in the hospital from a near-fatal attack. Charged with seven felony counts of assault with a deadly weapon, Brenda's husband pleaded innocent on all counts. In his defense he showed a birthday card Brenda had mailed to him after the beating. On it she had written, "You mean more to me than anything else in the world. I love you so very much, Sweetheart."

There must be many women who, after the first attack, simply pack their bags and walk out forever, and so are never included in any studies or statistics on wife battering. But obviously there are plenty who cannot or will not take the steps necessary to ensure they won't have to live in fear of violence or to stop their husbands' abusive behavior.

What causes a woman to stay with a man who batters and beats her? Some researchers suggest that women like Janet become involved in a violent relationship accidentally. Indeed, virtually any woman can be the victim of a single assault. According to the National Institute of Mental Health, it probably happens in as many as sixty percent of all American homes.

But it takes more than one assault to create what is known as the "battered wife syndrome." Whether or not the syndrome develops depends on what the woman does after that first time, and what steps she takes to make sure it won't happen again. If she is so overwhelmed with shock, humiliation, and fear that she withdraws to devote herself to making sure she doesn't set her husband off again, or if she makes excuses for his behavior, the chances are that the battering will continue. A battered woman is simply a woman who is unfortunate enough to marry an abusive man and then is unable to free herself from his violence.

NEITHER LOGICAL NOR SIMPLE

The real question, then, is this: What makes women stay with abusive men? When they do leave, why do they go back again and again? Why do so many wives continue to live under conditions of abuse that could very possibly lead to their death?

It doesn't make sense. It seems that it would be so easy for them to simply pack their bags and walk out. It certainly seems the logical thing to do. But the situations in which battered women become entangled very often do not lend themselves to either logic or to simple answers.

The stereotypical picture of a battered wife is that of a small, weak, worn-out, haggard woman who is completely dependent on her husband to support her and her flock of small children. She is usually thought of as poor, uneducated, and unskilled—a scared, passive woman who is used to living with violence. Because she stays with her husband, many people are convinced she enjoys being beaten—that for some reason she has a need to suffer.

Contrary to popular belief, most battered wives have not grown up in abusive homes. It is a minority of women who bring battered personalities into their marriages. But those who did grow up watching their fathers beat their mothers may conclude that all men beat their wives, that it is just something a wife has to accept and endure, that hitting is an acceptable expression of love.

Many battered women do fit one or another of these descriptions, but many others do not. Women who marry abusers come from all kinds of backgrounds—broken homes, happy homes and Christian homes, wealthy families and poverty-level families. Some are highly educated, others barely literate, some exceedingly talented, others not. Some are real beauties, others are quite plain. The only common denominator is that they all become battered women.

WHY DO BATTERED WOMEN STAY?

Many wives who stay trapped in abusive relationships do so because they are dependent on their husbands. They have been brought up to believe women are weak and inferior, that it is their duty to obey their husbands in return for a home, a family, and financial support.

Shocked and horrified at what is happening, such a woman may sincerely want to find a way out of her abusive circumstances. But if she has no money, no place to go for help and no job skills, what can she do? How can she support herself and her children? She may have no one to whom she can turn and no foundation for making a life of her own. She's caught between the proverbial "rock and a hard place." She sees no way out and so allows her husband to continue to batter her.

"Again and again I planned my escape, but I never went through with it," related Beth, a woman who stayed with her abusive husband for fourteen years, until he almost killed her. "When I sat down and really thought out my options, I knew it was dumb to even think escape was possible. Where could I go with no money? I couldn't just let my kids starve."

Yet upper-class women face a quandary, too. It is no easy matter for them to turn their backs on the affluent life to which

35

they have become accustomed and to face the prospect of a much more moderate lifestyle in today's competitive job market. Furthermore, they are well aware that their husbands' careers could be irreparably damaged if the violence were made public.

Fear prevents many women from escaping. "You can't hide from me!" Joan's husband threatened. "No matter where you go or how long it takes, I'll find you and I'll kill you."

For many of us, it is hard to believe that any man—certainly any Christian man—could make such a threat to his wife. It's even harder to believe he would actually carry it out. Yet we have a responsibility to proceed not only with Christian love and concern, but also with wisdom and caution.

As for Joan, she believes her husband will do exactly what he says. "I know he means it," she said in a trembling voice. "It's been three years since I finally left him, and I still can't sleep with the lights out. Some day he'll come after me. I'm sure of it."

Joan may be right. Police and FBI records indicate that thousands of women are killed and millions of others are severely injured by their husbands or boyfriends every year.[2]

Of the women who do leave their abusive husbands, an amazing percentage end up going right back to them. Very few of these returning women insist on a change in their husbands' behavior. Every time a battered wife unconditionally returns, she reinforces to her husband that he is the one in control, and he can do as he pleases to her.

Most battered women feel they somehow deserve the abuse. If they hadn't said or done the wrong thing, their husbands wouldn't have gotten so angry, they reason. Repeated beatings only intensify their feelings of worthlessness, incompetence, and guilt.

Some abused women are actually thankful their spouses are willing to "put up" with them. "How can I hate him?" asked Sara. "I must provoke him like he says I do. Obviously I'm doing something wrong. Somehow I've pulled him into this." After a few moments of silent tears she added, "He deserves better."

When a genuinely sorry husband sincerely promises his beaten wife that the abuse will never happen again, he is often forgiven. Although his wife has heard it all before, because she so badly wants it to be true, she agrees to give him "one more chance."

As Christians we are commanded to forgive. Yet if a battering husband is forgiven without any penalty for his behavior, he will almost certainly continue his abusive actions. Forgiveness must be coupled with an insistence that the batterer accept the consequences of his actions and that he take steps to ensure that it will not happen again.

Guilt may prevent a woman from leaving. This is especially true of a Christian woman. If she is at least partly to blame for his violent outbursts, how can she punish him? If she leaves, what will happen to him? And what about her reason for leaving— has she allowed her anger, perhaps her hatred, for him to win out over the forgiveness God has commanded of her?

Because the violence is often interspersed with periods of calm, battered wives often believe that the beatings won't happen again. They are able to maintain their hope that somehow they can do something to make those periods of love longer and longer and the periods of violence shorter and shorter. Unfortunately, experience shows that just the opposite is true: The periods of violence become longer and longer and the periods of love and tenderness shorter and shorter.

Still, even in the face of painful reality, many women continue to cling to the unrealistic hope that things will improve.

When talking about her abusive ex-husband, Liz insisted, "He wasn't always like that. There were times when we really had fun together. He was a real charmer and an awfully good companion. I guess that's why I stayed with him for so many years. The memory of those good times made me sure we could somehow work out our problems."

Debby recalled from her experience, "It got to where my husband was beating me almost every day. But every now and then he would stop pounding me for a little while. He would stay home and be nice to me and good to the children. Then I would close my eyes to the past and start to hope all over again."

"No one understands that there was once something in my husband that made me love him," explained Anita. "That part of him that I first fell in love with is something I cannot forget. It's still there somewhere, and when I see even a glimmer of it, I fall in love all over again."

Jackie had still another reason for staying with her abusive husband. Here is what she had to say: "From the very first my parents were against my marriage. They refused to cooperate with any wedding plans, so Gary and I eloped. I was just eighteen and my dad insisted I was too young to get married. He said if I was really in love it would last until I was older and more ready for marriage. The whole thing seemed so romantic—I thought Gary and I were just like Romeo and Juliet.

"When I called my parents to tell them we were married, my dad's only comment was, 'Okay, but from now on you're on your own. If things don't work out, don't come crying to us. You've made your bed, now you can lie in it.' How could I come crawling back two months later and tell them that Gary had started beating me?"

Many women feel their identity is tied up with their marriage. To them even a violent marriage is better than no marriage at all. Or a mother may be convinced that to break up the family would be bad for her children, that whatever the cost to her, the little ones need their daddy. Even when she sees the harmful effects of the abusive relationship on her children, she may still feel that having her husband in the home is better than their being fatherless.

A woman may cling to this "love" relationship because it is the only love she has. Most battered women suffer emotional and verbal abuse as well. Very likely her husband has convinced her that no one else would ever put up with her, that she could never find another husband, and that she could never find a decent job. The years of insults, put-downs, and beatings have taken their toll. Her self-esteem worn away, she has come to accept the image of herself as unlovable.

THE QUANDARY INTENSIFIED

For Christian women the dilemma can go even farther. If they see their suffering as just punishment from God for something they did years before, but for which they have never stopped feeling guilty, they are not likely to hold their husbands responsible for inflicting the pain.

Also many Christian women believe their husbands are *supposed* to control them, that it is a wife's duty to obey her husband in all things. Many wives are strongly urged to "forgive and forget" in order to keep the family together. They are told to save their marriages by examining their own faults, by becoming better wives, by learning to accept their husbands as they are, and by overlooking their husbands' weaknesses. This is wise counsel—except in a violent home.

When Christian women are married to abusive non-Christian husbands, they face yet another quandary: Are they responsible to bring their husbands to Christ? And if their husbands do become Christians, will the abuse stop and the problem be solved? Many think so. Sometimes it is someone else—the battered woman's family, friend, or minister—who emphasizes the importance of her role as a "savior."

As the years of emotional buffeting, violence, fear, and erratic cruelty take their toll, a victimized wife slowly begins to fall apart both psychologically and emotionally. She prays that God will change her husband, but change doesn't come. She becomes more and more passive, more and more unable to help herself. Her sense of self-worth long since shattered, she sees herself as incompetent and worthless, guilty and shameful. And since there seems no possibility of any other life for her, she feels powerless to make any changes. She not only feels trapped, but *is* trapped by her fear of leaving and terror of staying.

The world of a battered woman is a horrifying place.

1. "Flipside of the Japanese Miracle," *Alternative Press Digest* (no.3, 1975).
2. *Uniform Crime Reports for the U.S.* (Federal Bureau of Investigation, 1975).

4

PROBLEM?
WHAT PROBLEM?

"Why, Janet?" Lenore asked for the hundredth time. "Why?"

"It's not how you think it is," Janet insisted. "Roger loves me very much, and I love him. Why, just this morning he made me a delicious omelet and fresh-squeezed orange juice. And he served it to me in bed. How long has it been since your husband did anything like that for you?"

"He never has," Lenore replied coolly. "But then, he has never beaten me up either."

"Roger did not beat me up, Lenore!" Janet insisted. "It's just that he . . . well, sometimes he overreacts. That's just the way he is. Anyhow, it's more my fault than his. I always seem to end up doing things that bother him and make him angry."

"That's no excuse for doing what he did to you," Lenore retorted.

Janet leaned forward, and for the first time that morning she looked her sister straight in the eye. "Roger didn't mean to hurt me, Lenore. I knew he wasn't feeling well last night, yet I went right ahead and did something I knew would upset him. I'm like that, always disobeying him. I don't know why I do it, and I'm trying hard to stop. The thing is, he goes out of his way to do things to make me happy—things like breakfast in bed this morning—and yet I am too selfish to do the little things he asks of me."

After several minutes of silence Janet added, "Anyway, it won't happen again."

"And just what makes you so sure?" Lenore asked.

"If you had seen Roger this morning, you would understand. He was so sweet, so loving, so worried about me. It was almost as if last night was just a bad dream."

"A bad dream, was it? Then how do you explain the black eyes and bruises?"

Janet didn't try to explain. She just repeated, "Things will be different. You'll see."

DENIAL IS NATURAL

Will things be different for Janet and Roger? Not unless both face up to the fact that they do indeed have a problem. Even then change will require from both of them an enormous amount of work and determination, and a great deal of faith and love.

Janet's perspective seems unbelievable, yet for battered women denial is natural. It is especially easy in the beginning when the violence may not amount to much. It's not too hard to minimize striking out in a fit of anger or frustration. In fact, both husband and wife may be able to convince themselves that it never actually happened, or at least that it wasn't bad enough to be a real problem.

Janet needs a realistic assessment of what's been happening. She doesn't understand Roger nearly as well as she thinks she does. Like many battered wives, her view of her husband is badly distorted. While she idealizes his good traits, she closes her eyes to his bad ones.

"Roger didn't mean to hurt me," Janet insisted. "He didn't beat me up, not really."

How can Janet say such a thing? How can she believe it? Surely she can feel the pain! Yet even when she is presented with overwhelming evidence, Janet, like many abused women, cannot admit how bad her situation truly is, not even to herself.

Bent on maintaining her denial of reality, trying desperately to convince her friends and family—and herself—that what was going on was acceptable, Janet made endless rationalizations. Even though Roger's uncontrollable violence did not fit in with her "happy marriage" dream, she refused to give up hope that things would change. Giving up hope would mean admitting failure—her failure—and that was something she could not do. The periods of calm restored her optimism. After all, life was pretty good between beatings.

Because they grew up in violent homes, some battered women simply assume that a violent way of life is normal. They have no idea there are families out there who love and care for each other, families where husbands build up and encourage their wives, women who live without fear of pain and injury at the hands of their husbands.

But denial only perpetuates the problem.

"You made me do it," Roger told Janet. "It's your fault that it happened."

Said Kim, "My husband told me the beatings were my fault because I provoked him when I asked for grocery money and criticized him for spending a quarter of his paycheck on lottery tickets."

And like so many battered women, Janet and Kim believed what their husbands said.

SILENCE GIVES APPROVAL

And so did others. When her jaw was broken during a beating, the abuse Kim had been enduring for five years could no longer be hidden. Yet when it became known what was going on, again and again she was asked the same question by her family, her friends, and even her minister: "What ever did you do to make him do such a thing?"

But most people don't ask. Out of embarrassment and confusion, they simply ignore the bruises and injuries. Since they obviously cannot help seeing the marks of violence, their silence is interpreted as tacit approval.

"I felt worthless, totally to blame for what my husband was doing to me," Kim explained. "I kept thinking, *If I had done this differently or that differently, the beating wouldn't have happened. If I can just find the things that upset him and keep from doing those things, the problem will end.*"

Abusive men pick up on and encourage attitudes like this. If their wives are willing to assume the responsibility for their violent actions, so much the better.

THE BATTERING CYCLE

Thus many couples who are involved in abusive relationships manage to convince themselves that their families are normal, that there is a logical explanation for the violence. They know nothing of the vicious cycle present in most battering relationships. And because they don't understand the cycle, once it starts, few couples have any idea how to stop it. Certainly Janet didn't.

The battering cycle is made up of three stages. In the first, the tension begins and builds progressively. The man begins to get uptight, bothered by little things. After she has been through it a few times, his wife knows with dreadful certainty what is coming. Yet she tries to ward off the inevitable by doing everything in her power to keep things on an even keel. As the tension escalates, she tries desperately to preserve the peace by pleasing her husband in any way possible, or at least by staying out of his way. But it can't be done. The pressure becomes more and more oppressive and her efforts become less and less effective.

Knowing full well that a beating is coming, the woman becomes less able to react rationally. Finally, in a desperate attempt to retain some semblance of control, she may unconsciously provoke her husband just to get it over with. When this happens, her feelings of guilt grow stronger than ever. So do her husband's righteous indignation and his conviction that his actions are justified.

But in the end, what she does makes little difference. The time comes when the beleaguered wife loses all control over the situation. It is at this point that the second stage, the acute battering incident, takes over. The tension which has been steadily building up in the batterer grows too great to be contained, and he explodes in a fit of rage. Usually the actual violence is triggered by an incident remarkable only because it is so minor. Something as small as the table not being set correctly or an overdone roast may be all it takes. One man admitted that he broke his wife's jaw because "she wasn't looking at me right."

Once the attack starts, nothing the wife does can stop it. It is impossible to reason with an enraged man or to appeal to his better judgment. Begging, crying, pleading, and apologizing seem only to increase his fury.

Problem? What Problem?

And then it is over. In the wake of the storm both husband and wife feel a desperate need to make some sense of what has happened, to prove to themselves and to each other that everything is okay. And yet there is the nagging proof of blood and bruises and broken bones. It is hard to argue with the evidence. There is obviously a big difference between what they both know their relationship should be and the reality of what has just happened. The only solution is to minimize the episode and to rationalize the cause. He blames her, and she insists she was attacked only because he was angry or drinking or frustrated or tired.

Roger, the very picture of love and kindness, is typical of abusive men during this final stage. Many are loving, apologetic, even filled with remorse. To prove his love, the repentant man lavishes attention on his battered wife. He showers her with gifts and flowers. With heart-wrenching sincerity he swears that never again will he cause her pain. And his remorse is sincere. He truly believes he won't lose control again.

The loving respite stage lasts just long enough to rekindle the woman's flickering hope that this time perhaps things will be different. Maybe this time her husband will keep his promises. Maybe he really will change. Maybe from here on they will be able to live happily every after. But before long the tension once again starts to build, and all her hopes come crashing down. The cycle is starting over again.

Each time this cycle is repeated, the loving respite stage is shorter—in time it may disappear completely—and the acute episode grows more frequent and more severe.

What, then, is the answer?

The answer begins with facing the problem. The individuals involved, society, and the church need to admit that, yes, this *is* happening, and it must be stopped.

Only when one or both of the partners involved takes the first step of admitting that what is happening is wrong, and then makes a definite decision to do something about it, can the situation begin to change. Statistics regarding the reformation of abusers are grim. Yet, the answer for the believer lies in the transforming power of the Holy Spirit. After all, redemption is what the cross was all about.

5

"WIVES, SUBMIT TO YOUR HUSBANDS"

I t was a quiet evening. The children were tucked into bed, Roger was engrossed in the evening paper and Janet had just settled down with a glass of milk and a good book. The book lay unopened on her lap; Janet's mind was not on reading.

On the table beside her chair was a lovely bouquet of white roses, a gift from Roger this evening. "Just because I love you," he had said as he presented them. Their sweet fragrance permeated the room. Next to the roses was her favorite candy, a box of chocolate cremes he had brought home at noon.

Encouraged by these caring gestures and by the tranquillity of the evening, Janet summoned her courage and spoke the words she had rehearsed in her mind ever since Lenore had left. "I want to talk to you about what happened last night," she said softly.

Without looking up from his paper Roger replied, "Fire away."

"I don't understand what is happening to us, Roger. Please help me understand."

Carefully, deliberately, Roger folded the newspaper. Then he laid it down on the table next to his chair. "What do you mean, Dear?" he asked mildly. "I think we have a very good relationship, one we can be proud of. What exactly is it that you don't understand?"

Janet, trembling slightly, turned away from his steady gaze. Maybe she should not be bringing this up, not now when things were going so well. It could be that she was asking for a repeat of last night. Perhaps she should just drop the subject.

Roger was looking at her intently. "Well?" he pressed. "What is it you want to say?"

"You're a wonderful man, I know that," Janet began hesitantly. "You're a good Christian, a good father and . . . and a good husband. But there are times, Roger, times like last night . . ."

"Janet, you obviously don't understand the responsibility I carry," Roger interrupted. "It's not easy to be a good Christian husband. I love you, I really do. But you must understand that real love includes discipline. When you make mistakes you have to pay for them. You can see that, can't you?"

"Well, yes, but . . ."

"My mother respected my father, and I expect you to respect me," Roger continued. "It was my father who taught me that when a wife gets out of line, her husband has to straighten her out. It's not my idea, Janet. It's God's way. Do you want to argue with God's way?"

Janet said no more. What could she say? Roger was right. Who was she to argue with God's way?

ABUSE—A GOD-GIVEN RIGHT?

In her syndicated advice column, Ann Landers printed a letter from a man who called himself "Big Ed." The writer was responding to a previous letter in which a man had proposed wiring his wife's bedsprings so that at the press of a button she would receive enough of a shock to get her up in the morning to fix his breakfast.

"In principle he was perfectly right," Big Ed maintained. "Some women are like dumb animals. You have to show them who's boss. . . . I trained mine right from the beginning, and believe me, there are no arguments in our house. This is the way all families ought to be run."

Big Ed's show-the-dumb-animal-who's-boss attitude is bad enough, but Roger's position is even worse; what he does is done in the name of God. Roger steadfastly holds to the notion that a submissive wife should obey her husband unquestioningly and satisfy his every demand. Should she fail to do so, her husband has a God-given right to take any action he deems necessary to force her compliance.

THE DILEMMA OF THE BATTERED CHRISTIAN WOMAN

What's more, sincere Christian friends and advisers, in a misguided attempt to be consistent with Scripture, often admonish battered wives to go back home, to be more submissive and loving, and not to do things that stir up trouble. To support their counsel they point out such biblical passages as God's words to Eve in Genesis 3:16, "He will rule over you," or the Pauline admonition, "Wives, submit to your husbands" (Ephesians 5:22), or 1 Corinthians 7:4—"The wife's body does not belong to her alone but also to her husband."

"After my husband beat me severely for the third time in a month, I turned in desperation to my minister," said Pamela. "I wish I hadn't. First, he assured me my husband was not a bad man and meant me no harm. Then he instructed me to be more tolerant, more understanding, and to forgive my husband for beating me, just as Christ forgave those who beat him. I went home determined to do better, but I was greeted at the door by a punch in the face. How much must I tolerate? Does Christ really want me to stay in an abusive relationship?"

Christian women are indeed presented with a dilemma. They want to do what God would have them do, they want to obey the Scriptures, and they want the help and wisdom of those they respect as spiritual advisers. But they don't want to live their lives in fear and pain. While the abuse threatens them physically and psychologically, it also affects them spiritually.

When battered women seek help from what is often the only source of trained help—secular agencies—their confusion is intensified. Usually secular references condescend and accuse. They see Christian teachings as destructive traditions that doom women to live as second-class citizens.

A BALANCED VIEW OF SUBMISSION IS NEEDED

As followers of Christ, Christian women want to live by the principles laid down in Scripture. They want to understand where these principles fit into their own lives. They want to live after the example of Jesus.

From childhood many women have learned that subordination is biblical, that if they claim rights for themselves they are committing the sin of pride. Faced on the one hand with these teachings and on the other with the terror of an abusive husband, some women simply stop struggling and passively accept what they consider to be their fate. Others, unable to reconcile their dilemma, call it quits and turn their backs on the church.

When a Christian battered woman comes for counseling, very likely she will quickly be pointed to the scriptural references on submission. But when a woman is being beaten by the very one who is instructed to love her as Christ loves the church, what is she to do? Does God's word condone the kind of blind submission and subjection that can logically lead to the battering of wives by their husbands? Do husbands have the responsibility of disciplining their wives? Can battering be biblically defended? Absolutely not! A careful study of the Scriptures makes it abundantly clear that we can use neither God's word nor Jesus' example to justify wife abuse.

Although the Bible does not deal *specifically* with the problem of abuse, we can draw some conclusions on how we should respond to it by considering various scriptural principles on submission.

Before we go any further, let's understand exactly what submission is and what it is not. The *NIV Study Bible*, in its note on Ephesians 5:22, puts it this way:

> To submit meant to yield one's own rights. If the relationship called for it, as in the military, the term could connote obedience, but that meaning is not called for here. In fact, the word "obey" does not appear in Scripture with respect to wives, though it does with respect to children (6:1) and slaves (6:5).

Jo Berry, in her book *Beloved Unbeliever,* puts it this way:

> Submission is not blind obedience, although obedience is sometimes a byproduct of submission. Whereas obedience is following orders, submission is the voluntarily surrendering or yielding the will. . . . Obedience doesn't leave room for choice; submission does.[1]

In all of Scripture we see no example to support the contention that a man's position as head of the house allows him to physically abuse his wife. One important fact that is often overlooked is that submission is not a principle that applies only to women. Specific instructions regarding submission and subjection are given to children ("Children, obey your parents in everything, for this pleases the Lord"—Colossians 3:20), to citizens ("Everyone must submit himself to the governing authorities"—Romans 13:1), to husbands ("Husbands, love your wives, just as Christ loved the church and gave himself up for her"—Ephesians 5:25) and ultimately to every Christian ("Submit to one another out of reverence for Christ"—Ephesians 5:21).

Submission is required of all Christians (1 Peter 5:5). It is humility in practice. It is yielding to the leading of the Holy Spirit. It is an attitude of a Christ-centered life.

A BIBLICAL VIEW OF MARRIAGE

If we are prepared to commit ourselves to the authority of the Scriptures—whatever they teach, whether we like it or not—we must acknowledge the headship of the husband in the home. This is a clear and indisputable fact. It is scriptural. In their book *Liberated Traditionalism*, Ronald and Beverly Allen state:

> Because the man was created prior to the woman and because he gave her her name, he exercises a level of headship over her. But his headship is within a relationship of equals, for Genesis 1 has displayed that both the woman and man are bearers of the image of God, both are rulers over the earth. Mutually they share the tasks of sovereignty and majesty to the glory of God.
>
> This suggests a delicate balance: the woman is equal to the man, but the man is the head of the woman. With the fall, that delicate balance is lost. Now the woman resents even his loving headship, and the man responds as a brute, putting her in her place. Her desire is to lead the relationship; his is to lord it over her.[2]

In marriage, as in every other aspect of our lives, Jesus is our supreme example. The Apostle Paul tells us this in Ephesians 5:23—"For the husband is the head of the wife as Christ is the head of the church, his body, of which he is the Savior." An important question to consider is this: For whose benefit should the husband's headship be exercised? Is it for his own good, so that he can prove once and for all who's the boss? Not at all. Ephesians 5:23-27 tells us that the reason Christ loved the church enough to give his life for her was to make her holy, to be able to present her blameless. The very next verse begins, "In this same way, husbands ought to love their wives." His headship is for her benefit.

John Piper defines this further:

> So in this mysterious parable of marriage, the wife is to take her special cue from God's purpose for the church in its relation to Christ. Now to the husbands Paul says, take your special cue from Christ. . . . If the husband is the head of the wife, let it be very plain to all husbands that this means primarily leading out in the kind of love that is willing to die to give her life. . . . The husband who plops himself down in front of the TV and orders his wife around like a slave has abandoned the way of Christ. Jesus bound himself with a towel and washed the disciples' feet. . . . If you want to be a Christian husband you become a servant not a boss.[3]

And there is more. Besides loving their wives as Christ loves the church, husbands are given further instructions: "In this same way, husbands ought to love their wives as their own bodies" (Ephesians 5:28), "Husbands, love your wives and do not be harsh with them" (Colossians 3:19), "Husbands . . . be considerate as you live with your wives" (1 Peter 3:7). The Scriptures speak of the husband and wife as one flesh, and "no one ever hated his own body, but he feeds and cares for it, just as Christ does the church" (Ephesians 5:29).

God's pattern for marriage is clearly laid out in Ephesians 5:21—6:4. In this passage we see a picture of a husband who loves his wife with the deep, unselfish, self-sacrificing love that Christ himself has for the church. His wife willingly submits to him as head of the household. Their children, brought up in the training and instruction of the Lord, obey and honor their parents. It is a lovely picture of the Christian family as it is intended to be.

VIOLATION OF CIVIL LAW

In the study of submission, there is yet another law that must be considered. In Romans 13:1-5 we read that because civil authority comes from God, we are to be in subjection to it. Hebrews 13:17 admonishes us to "Obey your leaders and submit to their authority." In 1 Peter 2:13-14 we are again commanded to submit to "every authority instituted among men: whether to the king, as the supreme authority, or to governors, who are sent by him to punish those who do wrong." In short, we are to obey the law.

When analyzing the Christian's responsibility toward civil law, it becomes clear that Scripture does *not* teach absolute submission. John Piper addresses this concern well:

> The reason I say that submission means a *disposition* to yield and an *inclination* to follow is that no submission of one human being to another is absolute. The husband does not replace Christ as the woman's supreme authority. Therefore she must never follow her husband's leadership into sin.[4]

Christ never calls us to follow someone into sin, or to support them in their sin. We live in a country where the law clearly states that men are not allowed to batter their wives. Beating up on another person—and that includes a wife—is a felony. A man who physically abuses his wife is a criminal. Because he is breaking civil law, he is also breaking God's law.

And that's not all. Civil law requires that the crime of battering be reported. So anyone who fails to report the batterer's crime is also breaking God's law. This includes the beaten wife.

God's divine plan for Christians is to first submit to Christ, then to each other. In Titus 3:1 we read, "Remind the people to be subject to rulers and authorities, to be obedient, to be ready to do whatever is good, to slander no one, to be peaceable and considerate, and to show true humility toward all men." We know that in the marriage relationship he ordained that "the head of every man is Christ, and the head of the woman is man" (1 Corinthians 11:3) and that wives are to submit to their husbands (Ephesians 5:22).

This is God's divine blueprint for the structuring of Christian relationships. What we are not told is what to do when one falls out of line with his or her responsibilities. Fathers are instructed not to exasperate their children (Ephesians 6:4). If one disregards this instruction and abuses his little one, are we to consider it a matter between him and the Lord, or do we intervene on the child's behalf? Husbands are told to love their wives as Christ loved the church, to care for them and to treat them with gentleness. If instead a man beats and batters his wife, who has a responsibility to step in and put a stop to it? Wives are told to submit to their husbands, but if a husband takes advantage of his position, if his treatment of her is abusive and cruel, is she to continue to submit to the bitter end, or is there a point at which she should break with her husband?

Because we are not given specific answers to these questions, problems arise. But it must be noted that there is no example in Scripture where a woman is praised for submitting to the cruel abuse of her husband. What is demonstrated is that our Lord understands our humanity and takes pity on us. In Psalm 103:13-14 we read: "As a father has compassion on his children, so the Lord has compassion on those who fear him; for he knows how we are formed, he remembers that we are dust." Furthermore, Paul reminds us in 1 Corinthians 7:23 that "You were bought at a price; do not become slaves of men." All Christians—and that includes the wives of abusive men—should realize that their ultimate allegiance is not to any man, but to Christ.

A lack of balance in Christian doctrines has been partly responsible for the erroneous thinking that leads to wife battering. It is the duty and the responsibility of every Christian to study the Scriptures and to come to an understanding of the principles and values contained in them. It is not enough to place blind trust in authors and preachers and teachers and workshop leaders, however sincere and well-intentioned they might be. They can be wrong.

"Wives, Submit to Your Husbands"

Roger believed that he understood "God's way." He didn't. God's way is that marriage be a partnership of equals, each submitting in love to the other, each building one another up, each recognizing Christ as the head of their home. Roger does not understand what the Allens point out in *Liberated Traditionalism*:

> The lead sentence for the paragraphs on relationships is one of mutual submission: "Submit to one another out of reverence for Christ" (Ephesians 5:21). This verse colors all that follows. The verses that speak of the wife submitting to her husband (Ephesians 5:22-24) are in the context of the lead verse that demands submission by all. . . . The husband is the head of an equal. . . . For the genuinely biblical husband believes as much in the equality of his wife (Genesis 1) as he does in his headship over her (Genesis 2).[5]

Abusive violence may be an all too common pattern in marriage, but it cannot be justified by the teaching of God's Word.

1. Jo Berry, *Beloved Unbeliever* (Grand Rapids: Zondervan, 1981), p.42.

2. Ronald and Beverly Allen, *Liberated Traditionalism (Portland, Oregon: Multnomah Press, 1985)*, p.124.

3. John Piper, from his forthcoming book tentatively titled *Desiring God: Meditations of a Christian Hedonist* (Portland, Oregon: Multnomah Press).

4. Ibid.

5. *Liberated Traditionalism*, p.126.

6

AND THEN
THERE'S THE CHILDREN

At the first sound of crashing dishes and angry, yelling voices, five-year-old Christy had fled in terror to her big brother's room.

"Why does Daddy do it, David?" she had sobbed. "Why does he always have to hurt Mommy?"

Although David had no answers for his little sister, he knew exactly how she felt. He used to get scared and cry, too. But he wasn't so afraid any more, and Daddy had said he was too old to cry. So now he just listened. But as he listened the anger and hatred inside of him grew and grew until he sometimes felt as though it would swallow him up.

When the noises finally stopped, David had gone to bed, leaving Christy huddled alone in the corner. She hadn't gone back to her own room until the first light of dawn.

Janet knew her children were well aware of what she referred to as "the episodes." Although they never mentioned her bruises, she knew they couldn't help but see them. Once David told her, "My friend Kevin wants to be just like his father when he grows up, but I don't want to be like my Daddy. I'll never be like him!"

The little boy's words had been shocking enough, but the way he had said them—through clenched teeth and with hatred flashing in his eyes—had really frightened Janet. Yet as time went on, she was gradually able to push the incident farther and farther back in her mind. In time it was all but forgotten.

Young David meant it sincerely when he vowed never to follow in his father's footsteps. The question is, will he be able to keep his vow? Or will he grow to be a wife beater just like his father before him and his grandfather before that?

NO ONE UNTOUCHED

In an abusive home everyone suffers. As the violence reverberates throughout the family, no one is left untouched. But of the many casualties of family violence, the children's plight is the saddest of all. They suffer simply because they exist. And too often they suffer for a lifetime.

It's difficult to comprehend the life of children raised in an atmosphere of violence. Very early they learn that their home is different. They see that their friends' families are not like their own. Nor are television families or the ones they read about in their schoolbooks. They don't want to have their friends over. They can't look forward to weekends and holidays and vacations like other children do, because those are the times the abuse is likely to be worst.

Confused and worried, these children desperately need to share their hurts with someone. Yet they are too afraid and too ashamed to talk to anyone about it. In time the wounds of violence heal, but the scars remain forever.

OTHER ABUSE OFTEN PRESENT

When violence becomes a regular part of a family's life, it can take many different forms. In a home where the wife is abused, it is not unusual to find that the children are also being injured.

"When I got pregnant, I was sure my husband wouldn't hit me anymore," said Nancy, a shy, young wife. "Boy, was I wrong. He knocked me around more then than ever. And it really scared me because he was always punching me in the stomach. I couldn't understand it. He was so happy when I told him he was going to be a father—he seemed to want that baby. So why would he try to hurt it?"

For many abused wives the battering either starts or grows worse during pregnancy. And Nancy is right; a pregnant woman should be concerned about the effect the abuse will have on her unborn child. It may cause her to suffer a miscarriage, or her child could be born with birth defects or mental retardation.

Even a child who is perfectly healthy at birth isn't out of danger. Men who abuse their wives are likely to physically or sexually abuse their children as well.[1] This can mean slapping and hitting, or it can mean killing.

Nor is it always the father who makes the child a target for physical abuse. Sometimes a beaten wife who cannot retaliate against her husband takes her aggressions out on her child. Whether a child is singled out for suffering because he is blamed for his parents' problems, or whether he or she is injured during the course of the parents' fight, one thing is certain: A child unlucky enough to be born into an abusive family has a greater chance of being physically injured—or even killed—by his parents.

EFFECTS ON THE CHILDREN

"Roger is a good father to the kids," Janet had assured Lenore. "He would never do anything to hurt them. Except for his hitting me, we have a happy family, and I'm sure we'll be able to work out that problem. I know it's not the best situation in our home right now, but at least it isn't hurting David and Christy."

Is it possible to raise children in an abusive family without their being hurt? They are not always physically harmed, of course, but does that mean that there is no injury? Janet thinks so, and many others agree. But they are mistaken. Their children, even when they are not physically injured, suffer emotionally. Little ones who must watch and listen as their mothers are battered by their fathers can't help but suffer psychological scars.

Terror and pain so engulf and dominate the private world of many battered women that they can think of little else. They have little energy for their children. And so, even though they love their little ones dearly, and truly want what is best for them, their children are left to grow up without the supervision, physical care, and emotional support they need and rightfully deserve. Again, it is the children who suffer the most.

Even infants are affected by family violence. Very young babies will often show they're upset over the fighting and yelling at home by sleeping poorly and by being restless and nervous when they are awake. They are likely to cry easily, loudly, and persistently—the very kind of behavior that adds fuel to a battering father's rage and makes him still more abusive. A toddler shows his terror by screaming and crying, trying to hide, and by being unusually afraid of strangers, especially men.

Small boys often pick up the cue from their dads that "real" boys are good fighters and have loud, abusive mouths. However obnoxious they may become in their attempts to act like "real boys," they are inevitably torn emotionally by a nagging fear: What if someone should discover that, underneath all the bravado, they are just weak, frightened little boys after all?

As these children grow older, they often fail to learn, mature, and develop emotionally at a normal rate. Because they don't eat or sleep well, they may be ill much of the time. School-age children frequently suffer from physical problems such as asthma, recurrent headaches, and stomachaches. Many battle with a gnawing sense of guilt. They may be convinced that their parents' fights are all their fault, or that they are to blame for not protecting the mother. They may go so far as to try to intervene in the battles, begging the father to stop the beating or trying to push him away.

While growing up in a home controlled by a wife beater turns some children into frightened, guilt-ridden wrecks, it turns others into cruel mimickers of their fathers. After the age of five or six, many children, especially boys, begin to lose respect for their beaten mothers.[2] Instead of identifying with her, the child begins to identify with the aggressor. The time may come when a young person no longer cares about his mother's suffering. It simply becomes an accepted part of his family's life. One girl whose father was on trial for abusing her mother refused to testify against him. Instead she bragged, "My father can beat up anyone he wants to!"

Many have trouble expressing themselves and may resort to lying, stealing, fighting, talking back, destroying things, throwing tantrums, cheating in school, acting aggressively, trying to handle every situation with violence, blaming their problems on others, and experiencing a wide range of other behavior problems. These traits tend to make them unpopular with both adults and children. The normal problems of growing up are complicated by all the anger, guilt, and feelings of rejection and unloveliness that have become so much a part of them. Low self-esteem is almost universal. Poor school adjustment is common. The young person may be shy and withdrawn, or he may try to escape from his problems by turning to alcohol or drugs. Some begin to act in an increasingly aggressive manner by destroying property, by thievery, or by some other delinquent behavior. At first this aggression will be taken out on those who are smaller and weaker than himself—animals, perhaps, or younger children. But later it may well be turned toward other adults, perhaps even his own parents.

IMPOSSIBLE TO BE NEUTRAL

Teenagers find it almost impossible to remain neutral in their parents' battles. For some, running away from home seems to be the only escape from an intolerable family situation.

Many girls decide to get married in order to escape. Convinced that their own marriage will be much better than their parents', they find husbands as soon as possible. And how do they decide what a good marriage should be? All too often it is by watching those perfect television families. Many idealistic young girls are convinced that this is how their own relationships will be.

But television differs from real life. Their marriages, often to abusive husbands of their own, bear little resemblance to the romantic pictures of their dreams. Very soon these young wives become disappointed and discouraged. As they find themselves trying to deal with the unavoidable stresses and strains of marriage and motherhood, the vicious cycle begins anew, this time in their own families.

Teenagers who stay at home must choose one of two courses: either they support their mother, putting themselves at risk by trying to stop the batterer from hurting her, or they identify with the abuser and begin to support him. Imagine the battered woman's horror when she finds herself being attacked not only by her husband, but by her child as well!

Sometimes both the abuser and the victim are terrorized by their teenage children. And there are those parents who have been such good teachers, such effective examples, that their lives come to violent ends at the hands of their own abusive children.

What makes some kids willing to risk their own safety in an effort to help their mothers, while others go to the opposite extreme and join in on the abuse? The answer is simply an instinct for survival. In order to make it, a young person must adapt to the situation in which he finds himself. And as each one struggles to reconcile his own feelings with the unchangeable facts of life in his home, he does adapt in the best way he knows.

Some young people never come to terms with their situation. When a teenager can find no answers, no help, no end to his suffering, he may simply give up and quit trying. Pointing a loaded gun to his head or swallowing a handful of sleeping pills, he once and for all puts an end to his intolerable life.

Without a doubt the effects of domestic violence are devastating to those children who grow up under its influence. But the most frightening statistics are yet to be told. Study after study has shown that abused children are likely to grow into hateful, violent adults. A definite correlation exists between the violence children experience in their homes and the increasing violence in our society as a whole. Eighty to ninety percent of convicted felons in prison grew up in just such homes. Albert De Salvo, the notorious Boston Strangler, is one notable example. At his trial he described how his father beat him brutally, broke all his mother's fingers and knocked out her teeth. And then there are Lee Harvey Oswald, Sirhan Sirhan, and Charles Manson. Each of these men experienced a violent childhood. We must realize that today's abused children are likely to be tomorrow's criminals.

According to studies done in 1974 by Gelles, Steinmetz, and Straus, approximately eighty-five percent of the men who batter their wives, and thirty percent of their victims, grew up in violent homes.[3] Children who grow up watching dad's battering and mom's acceptance of it quickly learn that violence is an acceptable way to handle family problems. The way to get what you want is to bully, to take by intimidation or loud shouts or threats, to hit, or to throw things. As each abusive generation teaches the next generation to also live by violence, the vicious circle goes on and on and on.

Abusers are made, not born. And herein lies a real enigma. Even though he despises his traumatic childhood and vows again and again that he will never be like his dad, the chances are that the batterer's child will follow along in his father's brutal footsteps. Eventually his own marriage relationship will most likely be filled with the kicking, slapping, punching, bruises, and blood that he witnessed during his own formative years.

HELP CAN BE GIVEN

So here we have it—the facts of life as they exist for the children who grow up in abusive homes. Now the big question: Can anything be done to help children like David and Christy, or are they doomed to carry on the vicious legacy to which they have innocently fallen heir?

Before they can make a better life for themselves, these children must be taught that violence in a marriage relationship is absolutely unacceptable. Since they cannot learn this by the example they see at home, it may mean that their mother must be willing to take them and move out. That may be the only way to protect them. Battered women must be convinced of the necessity of this.

The Christian community can be effective here by encouraging concerned, sensitive adults to intervene in the lives of these emotionally needy children. Caring people can help them find their own strengths and resources, build up their self-esteem, establish lines of communication and encourage them to talk. By being a caring, loving friend with whom the child is welcome to share at any time, a person will be giving the child those things that will help him the most—a stable, loving, dependable person in his life, and a safe haven when things get too rough to handle. Fortunate is the child who has someone willing to listen to him, to care about him, and to believe in him.

Because the relationship these children see modeled at home is built upon violence and fear, it is vital that they have a chance to spend time in homes which are built on love and peace and mutual respect. Unless they see an alternative, how are they ever to learn that not all homes are like theirs, that there is a better way? (For more information on how children of

68

violence can be helped, both on an individual basis and in more general ways, see chapter 9).

The older a child is, the harder it will be to teach him new patterns of behavior or to help him learn to trust other people. But hard does not mean impossible. For some children professional help may be necessary. A wise, experienced counselor might well change a child's whole future. Many agencies are ready to provide this help at a price the family can afford. For information, call your local mental health agency or child welfare agency. (Also see Appendix 2 in the back of this book.)

On top of everything else, many young people are haunted by the specter of eventually carrying on the family tradition of battering and abuse. At the first sign of aggression in themselves, they worry that they are doomed to repeat the deeds of their fathers. They must be assured that this does not have to be so.

They need to realize that in the end, each person bears the responsibility for the direction his or her own life takes. Regardless of his background, the decision is in his own hands. Even though a person has inherited a legacy of violence, he does not have to keep it alive and pass it on to the next generation.

"My father always beat up on my mother," said thirty-one-year-old Paul. "He justified his actions by saying his father always disciplined his mother that way and his grandfather did the same to his grandmother, and all of them had happy, successful marriages.

"I never knew my grandmother, but my mother never seemed all that happy to me. And I can say one thing for sure: This is where the buck stops. I want my wife to love me, not fear me. I may not be the world's most perfect husband, but I'll say this: I've never laid a hand on her and I never will!"

1. Peter D. Scott, "Battered Wives," *British Journal of Psychiatry* (November 1974), pp.433-41.

2. Noor Van Crevel, "But What about the Kids?" a paper presented at the Conference of the American Sociological Association, August 1976.

3. Murray A. Straus, Richard J. Gelles, and Suzanne K. Steinmetz, *Behind Closed Doors: Violence in the American Family* (New York: Anchor Books, 1980).

7

GETTING OUT

At the sound of the crash, Janet hurried into the living room to see what had happened. She expected a knocked-over lamp or maybe a broken vase. What she found was Christy huddled in the corner behind an overturned table. Her little hands, covering her face, stifled her sobs.

"What happened?" Janet exclaimed when she saw the bruise forming on her little daughter's forehead.

"David hit me 'cause I was bad," Christy said through her tears.

Shocked and angry, Janet confronted her son. "David! How could you do such a thing to your sister?"

With a shrug David said matter-of-factly, "She wouldn't do what I told her to. I said to get my cars for me and she didn't, so I punched her."

Janet fell to her knees and embraced her sobbing daughter. What was happening to her children? David, only eight years old, felt perfectly justified in belting his disobedient sister. As for Christy—Janet cringed at the thought of her little girl cowering in the corner, helpless, wretched and ridden with guilt.

Then she suddenly understood. What she was witnessing was her own relationship with Roger being played out in miniature. It was a horrifying revelation. But worst of all, to these little ones it seemed perfectly normal.

"That's when I knew," Janet was later to say. "No longer could I let things go on the way they were. I can't tell you how terrified and ashamed and hopeless and guilty I felt at the idea of moving out of the home Roger and I had built together. But my fear for the children was even stronger."

The next day Janet packed up her children and two suitcases of clothes. After writing Roger an I-can't-go-on-like-this note, she drove to her sister's house. The three of them moved into the spare bedroom.

"I felt terrible about it," she admitted. "I believe in my commitment to Roger and here I was leaving him—breaking up our family. Lenore's house was crowded, and though she and her family were considerate and polite, I knew our being there was an imposition. The more I thought about Roger's tirades and beatings, the less terrible they seemed. Even the horror I had felt over what had happened between David and Christy began to fade.

"And then there was Roger. He was shocked and hurt to think I would really leave him. He telephoned me constantly, and sent me the sweetest cards and letters telling me how much he missed me and the children and how lonely he was. He said he was sorry for what had happened, but he also insisted that I had to share the blame.

"Someone had given Roger the name of a Christian counselor, and he suggested that we go together to see the man. Nothing could be worked out, Roger insisted, until the children and I came back home. Then he informed me that the future of our family was in my hands, that I alone was responsible for what happened to us."

It was several minutes before Janet spoke again. "It wasn't always bad, you know. We had some really happy times together, Roger and me. Despite all that had happened, I couldn't help remembering the good times." After another pause she added softly, "The more I thought about it, the more lonesome I became. Even with all those people in the house, I felt so alone. I missed Roger. Before the week was over, the children and I moved back home."

JOLTED INTO ACTION

It takes courage, decisiveness, and every bit of energy she can muster for a battered woman to seek help and counseling. The very act of seeking help can be deadly dangerous, and battered women know it.

Still, there are those who do leave. Pushed and driven by despair, by fear for their children, or perhaps by a "last straw" attack, some women at last are ready to turn their backs on the abuse they have suffered. They begin the long, arduous task of picking up the pieces and trying to salvage lives for themselves and their children.

73

Janet's commitment to her marriage is what motivated her to endure Roger's physical and verbal abuse. Besides, she had a nagging fear that it was she, not Roger, who was at the heart of the problem. If that were so, she had a responsibility to hang in and work things out. Not until she was confronted with the undeniable evidence of emotional damage in her children was she jolted into taking action.

IS SEPARATION BIBLICAL?

"He may not be much of a father," Susan said of her violent, alcoholic husband, "but any father at home is better than no father at all." As with Janet, what keeps many battered women from leaving is a strong belief that commitment to marriage and husband leaves no option but to live with him. Unfortunately, "For better or for worse, till death do us part" is too often taken to mean "stay in your marriage, even if it kills you!"

"I talked to my minister about Tom's behavior," Susan related, "but he wasn't very sympathetic. He said I should go home and pray and be careful not to upset Tom. According to him, it was my job to work out the difficulties. I should be willing to endure the suffering and hold the family together. He insisted that if I were to leave home, it could only lead to divorce, and that would be going directly against the Bible."

This sincere conviction that a marriage must be preserved at all costs presents an enormous problem to battered women. Like Susan's minister, many Christians believe that separation is tantamount to divorce, and that makes it unacceptable for Christians.

The liberalized attitudes toward divorce on the part of so many Christians are sad indeed. "Easy" divorce in Christian circles has caused tragic results. Divorce is *not* God's way.

The Bible's teaching concerning divorce is specific and authoritative; it's hard to argue with since it comes from Christ himself. Fundamentally, the principle is that once a couple is married they are to remain one: "What therefore God has joined together, let no man separate" (Matthew 19:6).

Does this mean a battered woman who removes herself from her home is guilty of separating what God has joined together? Not at all. To stay in a violent situation in an effort to preserve the family is foolish. By the very act of violence, the marriage pattern as set up in the Bible has already been disrupted. Leaving the danger zone and working toward healing the relationship may be the only action that can prevent the two that God has joined together from being torn asunder.

There is something very disturbing about a Christian counselor who, when confronted by a battered wife, has nothing to offer but counsel to pray about the situation. It is our responsibility as Christians to confront sin when we see it—and wife abuse is certainly sin. To encourage a woman to stay in an abusive situation is circumventing our responsibility to be redemptive. The teaching on Christ's view of marriage must include his admonition against divorce as well as his teachings on God's love, the sanctity of life, and the responsibilities of husbands to wives and wives to husbands.

In 1 Corinthians 7, Paul gives several instructions to Christians about what their conduct should be within the marriage relationship. He starts out by reaffirming Jesus' teaching:

> "To the married I give this command (not I, but the Lord): A wife must not separate from her husband." (1 Corinthians 7:10)

But understanding that there are Christian wives who are involved in family relationships that have deviated far from what they were intended to be, Paul went ahead and added:

> "But if she does, she must remain unmarried or else be reconciled to her husband." (1 Corinthians 7:11)

It is not the purpose of this book to attempt to make a theological statement concerning divorce and remarriage. Many good, biblically based books have been written on that topic. But when the issue is wife battering, divorce is not really the point. Leaving the home to find safety from a husband by no means needs to lead to permanent separation or divorce. The important thing is that the abused woman whose life or well-being is in danger must be allowed—no, encouraged—to get out. Once she has taken that step, she can seek to reconcile her husband by confronting him, by seeking help from others, and by insisting upon his need to change. (For more options, see chapter 9.)

TOUGH LOVE IS NECESSARY

Like Janet, a wife will often leave after a severe beating or a scare about her children's welfare. But soon her husband shows up, sad and ever so sorry, full of love and apologies. He promises he will change and begs her to come back. And it's not just an act. He genuinely does regret what has happened. Usually the woman returns home, only to see the apologies and promises forgotten. Before long the abuse starts up again.

"Years ago I knew I should leave Dick," said Marian of her husband of twenty years. "It would have been best for me and it would have been best for my children. But I loved him then and I love him now. That love makes it impossible for me to leave him."

Marian is wrong. While loving an abusive man will surely make it hard to leave him, in the long run leaving could well be the most loving thing an abused wife can do. Very often it is the very act of leaving that finally forces such a man to face the reality of what he is doing. Dr. James Dobson would call this "tough love."

"I want to say a word to the women out there whose husbands are abusing them," a man who called himself "Regrets in Oregon" wrote to columnist Ann Landers. "Get counseling at once. If he doesn't stop, leave. My wife took too much for too long."

But certainly this is easier to say than to do. Even when a woman has a fairly clear idea of the consequences of continuing in her relationship, there can be a giant step between that realization and her decision to act on it.

Abused wives become entrapped in a vicious, no-win contest. Yet many experts insist that a long-suffering partner of an abuser is actually the catalyst that keeps the conflict going. She tries so hard to be a "good" wife—always ready to forgive, always willing to cover for her husband's actions, always the martyr determined to change him. The tragic outcome of this fierce, unpredictable relationship is that neither husband nor wife accepts the responsibility for their actions. And in the end, nothing changes.

In battering relationships things do not just get better. Abused women need to understand this reality. If a woman wants her husband to change, she must take action. That is her responsibility. Even though it means making herself and her husband vulnerable, she must stop hiding her situation. She must admit it to herself, she must trust others with the knowledge, and she must enlist their help.

She must understand that her husband will never change unless he gets help. And he likely won't agree to get that help unless he is forced into it by fear of exposure, of punishment, or of losing his wife and children. An abused woman must realize that the only way she can help her husband is by forcing him to recognize the serious consequences of his actions. Ironically, it may take the threat of separation to bring him to the place where their marriage can be saved.

QUESTIONS COMMONLY ASKED BY BATTERED WOMEN

Difficult though it may be, a battered woman should leave. Even without immediate danger, many experts suggest that if this is the third instance of abuse, a pattern is forming and she should leave.[1] Left unchecked, that pattern will surely get worse.

1. What are my options?

You have several:

(a) You can decide to stay. This means staying home and keeping quiet, carefully guarding everything you do and say. If you choose this, you will be the eternal conciliator. But do understand, no matter how passive you become, in time you are sure to trigger your husband's anger. Even worse, you will pay a terrible price emotionally for living a time-bomb existence year in and year out.

Getting Out

If you choose to live with the constant threat of violence, you should be prepared to do anything necessary to avoid upsetting your husband. You will need to be constantly on your guard. When you are hit you must not hit back. Doing so will only infuriate him further. Realize that by staying you are in effect agreeing to live according to his terms—why should he change?

Since you will be living in a constant state of uncertainty and potential danger, it is vitally important that you establish a support system of people upon whom you can call in a crisis.

To continue to accept victimization is certainly an option, one that is chosen by many battered women. Because it requires the least action, it is the easiest choice to make. It is also the most dangerous and the one that is the least likely to effect change in your husband's behavior. Not only can it put your life in danger, but your children will continually be damaged by having to witness the violence committed against you. As time goes on, the abuse will almost certainly become more frequent and severe.

You should do everything you can to keep your children in as sane and stable an environment as possible. But that doesn't mean you should lie to them and tell them all is well when it clearly isn't. They are the ones who see you beaten, hear you scream, and watch you cry. Imagine their confusion if you insist nothing is wrong!

Your children need to know they are not responsible for what happens between you and your husband, that they cannot stop the fighting or protect you. Since they are growing up seeing violence as the normal way of solving problems, they must be carefully taught there are other ways to deal with people, ways that don't involve hurting them. And they must understand that these methods are far better than what they see at home.

Give your children explicit instructions as to what they are to do when you are attacked. Should they run to a neighbor's house? Should they call the police? Should they lock themselves in the bathroom? Whatever you tell them, make them understand that they must never intervene during an attack. While it is sweet and noble for a child to want to protect his mother, it is also extremely dangerous.

(b) You can determine you will change your husband. This knowledge may come hard, but you cannot change him. Change comes hard, and unless it is your husband's decision, it doesn't come at all. He must accept the responsibility for his behavior and any new course it will take.

If you decide to stay and work for improvements in your marriage, you can begin by trying to communicate with your husband, to share your concerns, your fears, and your dreams with him. But do be realistic—it is unlikely your efforts will make much difference.

Whatever your husband's response, you should work to help your children understand—though certainly not to accept—the problem in your home. They must learn that violence is wrong and must be stopped. You should also get counseling. Even though your husband will probably refuse to go along, you and your children will need it.

As in the first option, you, too, should create a network of people around you who can give you support and help.

As for helping your husband toward healing, you can try to force him to face the consequences of his actions. Stop covering up for him.

(c) You can decide to leave. Remember, rather than breaking up your marriage, your departure may be what can save it.

If you decide to make some positive changes in your life, begin by sitting down with your husband when he is in a good mood and telling him straight out, "I won't let you do this to me ever again." Carefully lay out exactly what it is that you refuse to tolerate, and what you will do if he does it. (Remember, though, don't make threats that you will not, or cannot, carry out. This will only make matters worse.) If the violence does happen again, or if your husband's response is threatening, pack your bags and leave.

2. But what exactly should I do?

You should carefully and honestly assess the situation.

Getting Out

Based on that assessment, you will have to make basic decisions. Here are some guidelines to help you.

- Admit that there is a problem. Unless you do, nothing will change. You may be embarrassed about the battering, and worried about what people will think of you for having gotten involved in such a relationship in the first place. Your feelings are understandable. Perhaps it will help to remember you are not alone. Thousands of other women are also suffering at the hands of their husbands. You have no reason to be ashamed.

- Speak up. Others can't help you if they don't know you need help.

- Stop blaming yourself. You cannot change your husband's behavior. Your situation probably won't be resolved until you understand that the violence is his problem.

- Look to God for guidance. It is your privilege— and your responsibility—to discuss this matter with the Lord. James 5:13 instructs us: "Is any among you suffering? Let him pray." That is not to say that prayer is a substitute for action, however. God wants you to take responsibility and make decisions. He wants you to trust, but there are times when he also wants you to act.

- One of the first decisions you must make is to determine exactly how much abuse you are willing to take from your husband. Will you endure three beatings? Five? Ten? Will your limit be a broken bone? Or injuries severe enough to require hospitalization? Whatever it is, once that limit is set you should make a commitment to leave the minute your husband steps over that line.

- Take advantage of times of relative calm or tenderness to tell your husband how you feel about what is happening to you. It's possible that he may honestly think he has a right to do what he is doing. Or he may never have considered the consequences of his actions. Either way, he needs to know that he is causing you real pain, and that he is building up anger and resentment within you.

- Prepare for an emergency. In case of an attack, your first concern should be to get yourself and your children out of the house. In order to provide yourself with some degree of protection, you should take the precaution of hiding extra money, spare car keys, and important documents. The hiding place you choose should be secure, yet accessible enough to allow you to get what you need in a hurry. The phone number of the police department should be kept handy, and you should have a place to go should you have to leave home suddenly.

- If you have been hit, it's a good idea for you to see a doctor immediately. Not only might your injuries be more serious than you think, but the doctor can provide written, professional proof of the abuse you have suffered.

- Take control of the situation. You badly need to be in charge of your own life. Your first and most important step to achieving this goal is to start making your own decisions. You can be in control. Do it!

- Be willing to accept help. It's available for you. Look to your friends and relatives, your church, and your pastor.

  You might also arrange to meet regularly with two or three Christian friends just to talk and pray together. It will help to have someone in whom you can confide, someone who will support both you and your husband in prayer.

  While friends can lift your spirits and hasten your recovery, there is a limit to what nonprofessionals can do. You may need more than just a friend; you may need a trained counselor.

Finding the right counselor might take some real doing, but it is worth the effort. Your pastor or friends can be your best source of referrals. When someone makes a suggestion, try to find out what he or she liked about the counselor. With what problem did the counselor help? What special qualities does the counselor have? Are they the qualities that are important to you? For other counseling possibilities, look in the telephone book Yellow Pages for agencies which work with battered women, or for those who may be able to make referrals.

Before you commit yourself to a specific counselor, interview him or her by telephone. Ask questions about cost, experience in working with battered women, and what special training he or she has in the field of domestic violence. It is important you choose someone who understands the complexities of wife abuse and whose theology you respect.

- Use whatever community resources are available to you. Don't be too embarrassed or too proud to apply for food stamps or aid to your dependent children. Helping people over the rough times in their lives is the purpose of public assistance. If you are eligible for social service intervention or financial aid, apply for it.

To find out about the services available in your community, get in touch with the local YWCA, family service agency, crisis hotline, your pastor, or the police emergency department. Check the Yellow Pages under "Women's Shelter," "Crisis Intervention," and "Domestic Violence." Also check Appendix 1 in the back of this book.

- Consider getting legal counsel. This may not be necessary for you. Then again, it may be. Should your husband threaten to sue for custody of your children, or to leave you without financial support, good legal advice will clarify what your rights are. If you cannot afford a lawyer, you can apply for free or reduced fee legal counsel.

3. When should I leave?

At any point, whether or not you should leave is a decision only you can make. For many battered women it's not an easy one. In general, you should leave if:

- The abuse occurs three or more times. Authorities on the subject agree that when the abuse occurs three times, it constitutes a pattern. When a pattern is established, the violence almost never improves on its own. It only gets worse.

- The beating was severe, even if it was the first offense. How severe is severe enough to force you to flee is something only you can decide. Did you have to be hospitalized? Were any bones broken? Did your husband use any potentially deadly weapons?

- Your life has been threatened, either by word or by the severity of the attacks. It is not safe to stay with a man who threatens your life.

- You have set limits on what you are willing to take and your husband steps over that line. If you don't follow through on your ultimatum, your husband will believe you are not serious about insisting he stop his violence.

4. Can I ever go back?

Of course you can. Moving out of your home doesn't mean you have to stay away, nor does it mean you have to get a divorce.

Many women who leave abusive husbands find themselves confused. If they refuse to go back home, they are accused of being unreasonable and unforgiving, of being unwilling to work out their problems and to help save their marriages. They may also be accused of not trusting God to change their husbands. On the other hand, if they do go back they could well be returning to the same violence from which they managed to escape.

Don't allow yourself to be pushed into returning home too soon. When and if you do go back, it should be when you are sure your husband will no longer batter you. You cannot help your husband or repair your marriage by returning home to be beaten again. You can accomplish these ends only by forcing your husband to recognize the serious consequences of what he is doing. It may take the threat of a permanent separation to bring him to this point. Or it may be that nothing will.

Divorce is not God's way. One has only to read Mark 10:1-12 to see that. God never intended marriages to end that way. Some marriages will end in divorce—your husband may deny his need to change and if you refuse to return home, he may threaten to divorce you. Again, tough love is one that does not condone sin.

5. Where can I go?

The next question is this: When I leave, where should I go? Friends and relatives are possibilities, of course. And for many this is the best answer. But in some cases there is the distinct danger that a man will search out his wife and present a threat to anyone who is sheltering her. Obviously, if he has made such a threat it would be unfair to put someone else in danger. For this reason, and because many women have no close friends or relatives to whom they can turn, safe houses or shelters have become the cornerstone of support services for battered women who leave their homes.

Shelters do more than just shelter. They are places of transition. While there, battered wives receive encouragement and support. They are taught how to survive. A good shelter also provides counseling, personal necessities such as food and clothes, transportation, help in locating permanent housing, assistance in finding a job or job training, and access to advocacy and legal advice.

It is a fortunate woman who finds a shelter which operates in a Christian context, one that supports the sanctity of marriage and a desire to help the abuser as well as the abused. Unfortunately there are precious few of these around. (See chapter 10 for more information about what the church can do to meet this need.)

Whether she seeks refuge with a friend or relative or goes to a shelter, the *initial* concern of a Christian battered woman is no different than that of a non-Christian battered woman. She wants to protect herself and her children. However, this concern is coupled with an equal concern to bring about repentance and reconciliation with her husband.

The Christian response to an abusive relationship is to stay open to the possibility of a reconciliation and to pray toward that end. If her husband is not a believer, the woman *should* desire his salvation and the reestablishment of their life together on a more solid ground. *But a goal of reconciliation does not negate the need to leave an abusive situation.*

For a battered woman, the best advice is this: *If you are in danger, or if the abuse you are suffering is out of control, get out.* If possible, find a friend or relative to help you. Turn to other Christians. Get to a hospital if you are hurt. Take your children with you.

If you are a victim of severe or repeated abuse, the idea of leaving probably scares you. That's to be expected. But don't let your fear stop you. Go anyway. Arrangements can be made, problems can be worked out later, options can be explored and questions can be answered. Your present concern is the safety of yourself and your children, plus a loving step of action that can immediately help your husband begin the long process of change. Go!

1. Lenore Walker, *The Battered Woman* (New York: Harper and Row, 1979).

8

THERE ARE LAWS, YOU KNOW

For over a month things were better between Janet and Roger. Irritations did occur—an evening's dinner ruined when the meatloaf burned, an overflowing washing machine and flooded kitchen—but Roger took everything in stride. He was trying hard to make it work. So was Janet. She took great pains to keep things on as even a keel as possible.

Together they went to see a counselor, one recommended by their pastor. During their first meeting everyone was calm and polite, and Roger held his wife's hand throughout. After listening to them for a while, the counselor assured Janet that Roger meant her no real harm.

"You folks will be fine," he promised. "You just need to learn a bit more about the give and take of marriage. Try to be more considerate of each other, more tolerant and understanding."

After a couple of sessions Janet and Roger agreed that the counseling wasn't worth the cost.

"Everything is fine now," Janet told herself. "The problem is behind us."

Then one Friday night, their happy new beginning came to an abrupt, shattering end. It happened so fast, so unexpectedly, that it almost cost Janet her life.

It had been a bad day all around. David and Christy, both home from school with colds, were grouchy and demanding. Even so, Janet had worked hard to prepare a nice dinner for her husband. But when dinner time came, Roger wasn't home. As she watched the clock and waited, Janet grew more and more upset. By the time he finally arrived—almost two hours late— the roast was dried out, the vegetables overdone, and Janet had a pounding headache.

Roger had not had a good day either, and he was in no mood to listen to Janet's complaints. Had things not been going so well for so long, Janet would have sensed danger and been on her guard. But she was so sure everything was different now that she forgot to be careful.

"You could have called me to let me know you would be

late," she snapped as Roger walked into the house. "I've had a terrible day, my head aches, and now dinner is ruined!"

Roger informed her his day hadn't been so great either.

"The kids are driving me crazy," Janet continued. "Why don't you go upstairs and read to them for a while? I need some rest."

Roger replied that he could use a rest himself. Besides, he added, Janet was their mother and mothering was her job.

"Well, it wouldn't hurt you to lift a hand around here once in a while," she shot back. "I'm not their only parent, you know!" As an afterthought she added, "And since you chose to show up so late, you can warm up your dried-out dinner yourself. The children have already eaten and I'm not hungry!" With that she stomped out of the room.

Janet made it as far as the hall before Roger caught up with her. Grabbing her by the shoulder, he jerked her around. At that moment, when she caught sight of his rage-twisted face, she first realized her danger. But by then it was too late.

Roger's hands closed around her throat. Though she struggled desperately to free herself, he was too strong for her. She tried to scream, to beg, to plead, but no sound came out. She struggled, she kicked, she hit, but to no avail. In her last moments of consciousness, Janet wondered who would care for her children after she was gone.

The next Janet knew, she was laying on the hall floor where she had fallen. She could hear Roger banging dishes around in the kitchen. Silently, hardly daring to breathe, she eased herself to the bedroom. Still sitting on the floor, she reached for the phone, then dialed.

"Hello, Police?" she whispered. "I need help . . . No, it's not an intruder. It's my husband. He just tried to kill me!"

A HANDS-OFF ATTITUDE

A battered woman who comes to the end of her endurance has no choice but to reach outside for help. For most, it is an act of desperation, one taken with great reluctance. Typically, it has taken her a long time to work up the courage to cry out for help.

In all fifty states, what Roger did to Janet is a felony. Although most do not have a crime specifically known as "wife beating" or "spouse abuse," the criminal codes do include related crimes—assault, battery, aggravated assault, and intent to assault or murder.

And yet battering persists because many people believe it's all right for a man to hit his wife. They think laws against attacking others don't apply when a husband beats his wife "to teach her a lesson," or even to let out his frustrations and pressures.

It was nine o'clock when Janet called the police. At nine thirty they still had not come. At nine forty-five they called back to ask if she still wanted them. But by then Roger was contentedly settled in his favorite chair in front of the television set, and Janet, exhausted and hurting, was ready for bed. She told them to forget it.

No one asked if she was all right. No one suggested she see a doctor. No one gave her any guidelines as to what she should do if she were attacked again.

Often police are reluctant to get involved in so-called "family problems." Elaine can testify to that. For years she was a battered wife. Even though the police were confronted with blatant proof of her husband's physical abuse, she found them unresponsive to her repeated appeals for protection.

"They kept telling me it was just a family spat," she said. "They would take my husband out and talk to him, then come back and tell us to shake hands and make up. Even now, years later, I get furious just thinking about it! I mean, if my husband had slapped anyone else around the way he did me, he would have been arrested in a minute."

Police have good reason for being reluctant to respond to such calls. Domestic violence can be lethal, and not only to the battered women. A 1978 article in *Police Magazine* reports that forty percent of all police deaths on duty are the result of becoming involved in a family dispute.[1]

Not only are these cases dangerous, but they are also extremely difficult to resolve because usually they are charged with irrational emotion. Police and prosecutors argue that many women file charges just to teach their husbands a lesson. When they feel their point has been made, they drop the charges.

Some police departments do not require their officers to respond to domestic violence calls at all. Others assign them such a low priority that the callers can wait for hours for someone to arrive.

Elaine's story is a good example of what often happens when the police do come. The woman is told of the difficulties of pursuing a legal prosecution and of the trouble it will cause. The policemen quiet her down, talk to her husband, and leave. In the end, she has received no real help at all. Again, the lack of confrontation reinforces her husband's position. He reasons that if he were *really* breaking the law, the police would have arrested him. When the police leave, he feels free to continue the beating.

Sometimes, of course, the police do make arrests, especially if they actually witness the abuse. Even so, there is no guarantee that the courts will take strong action against the abusing husband. The abuser may well be let off with only a warning not to do it again.

It would seem that the legal system offers greater protection to the batterer than to his victim. As Elaine pointed out, how is it that a crime—which would surely be punished if committed against a stranger—is winked at when it is committed by a husband against his wife?

Unfortunately, this is in keeping with tradition. For centuries the legal system has allowed husbands what is called "the right of chastisement" over their wives. While laws have changed in the last hundred years, attitudes haven't. Police and the courts are reluctant to get involved in situations within the home. It is un-American, they feel, for the government to intrude upon families.

So that's where the police find themselves. They are criticized if they "interfere" in a family squabble, and if they don't they are criticized for not protecting the victims. No wonder they have taken the stance that most incidents of wife abuse are private matters that are best worked out by the couple involved.

This "hands-off" attitude by those who support "the sanctity of the home" and shun interference in domestic affairs has produced a dangerously difficult situation for battered women. "It wasn't until my husband almost killed me with a knife that my pleas were finally taken seriously," Elaine related. "When the police asked me what I wanted done, I told them I didn't want my husband in prison, I just wanted him kept away from me."

Elaine's is an extreme situation. Certainly not every batterer will go to such lengths. Yet it must be remembered that a man caught up in an abusive rage often loses the power to control his violence. And so, even though Elaine's plight may be difficult for Christian readers to accept, it is important to realize the possibility of deadly violence. It does happen.

Elaine soon found that even keeping a husband away can be hard to do. It's not that it can't be accomplished legally. It can. But papers, however legal, are not necessarily enough to actually keep a husband away from his wife.

Despite what seems to be the failure of the system, some legal experts contend that the laws, if enforced, would be sufficient to protect battered women. But often they are not enforced. Insisting upon and following through with the arrest and prosecution of batterers is terribly difficult and discouraging for abuse victims. Even when they do persevere, convictions have traditionally been few and sentences unrealistically light. But things are beginning to change.

RECENT LEGAL CHANGES

Recent legal changes, plus a new public awareness and concern for the plight of battered women, indicate that help is at last on the way. To date thirty-four states have passed laws making civil protection orders available. Under many of these laws a judge can order a batterer to abstain from beating his wife, to move out of their home, to stay away from her, to attend counseling sessions or even to pay support or restitution. And these orders are being enforced. In some states an abuser who violates a civil protection order may be subject to arrest without a warrant and to criminal penalties.

One of the first programs to recognize that domestic violence is not a private matter, but a crime, and that it should be prosecuted as such, was established in Los Angeles. Under this program the decision to prosecute was taken out of the victim's hands. Should an abused wife decide to drop the charges against her husband, she is told that the matter is no longer in her hands. The charges stand.[2]

This concept has spread. In Michigan, a law passed in 1978 allows police to arrest batterers for misdemeanor assaults on grounds of "probable cause." This law has since become a model for other states. In Massachusetts, a woman can walk into any court and receive an immediate emergency restraining order to protect herself against an abusive husband.

A higher conviction rate is one result of the tightened laws against wife beating. The idea is to let batterers know that their behavior is not acceptable and will not be tolerated. A brush with the law can indeed have a sobering effect, causing a man to stop and think hard about the consequences of his actions.

A conviction for wife battering also helps restore the victim's perspective on who is to be blamed for the abuse. If the courts declare that the violence is wrong and that the batterer is responsible for his own actions, battered women are less likely to keep blaming themselves for the abuse.

WHAT SHOULD I DO WHEN ATTACKED?

That's not to say that filing criminal charges against a violent spouse is always the best course of action. Before a woman does so, she should weigh several factors. While it may serve as a deterrent to future abuse, and while it does punish the abuser for his violent behavior, it can also have some definite drawbacks.

There Are Laws, You Know

For one thing, the criminal process is a slow one. If the abuser is released on bail-pending trial, he may be angry and embarrassed enough to attack his wife again. And then there is the problem of finances—attorney and court fees, and having to get along without the jailed man's income.

It is important to be informed, to know the basics of the law and to understand the realities of what is likely to be encountered. But if you are a battered woman, the question you probably are most interested in having answered is this: When I'm attacked, what should I do? The following points will help you make some necessary decisions.

Decide whether or not you would be better off with or without the intervention of the police. Do you think that the shock of being confronted with the seriousness of his actions by a law enforcement officer will jar your husband into recognizing what he is doing to you? It may. Are you afraid for your life? If so, you need protection. Are you willing to leave the house, even if it is only for a short time, while your husband cools off? If you have some place to go, the police will take you there.

When you call the police, be specific. Tell them exactly what is happening to you. Explain your situation briefly but completely. Say that it is an emergency. If your husband has a weapon, say so. If an officer doesn't show up within a few minutes, call again.

When the police arrive:

- Stay as calm as you possibly can.

- Whether or not an arrest is made, insist that they make a report. It will be proof of what happened to you.

- Tell them about the assault in detail. Their report should describe any weapons your husband had. Don't limit this to guns or knives. It may have been a frying pan, a lamp, shoes, a hammer. Anything that is used against you qualifies as a weapon.

- Show the officers any injuries or bruises your husband has inflicted on you. If the policemen suggest that you get medical help, do so. They can take you to an emergency room.

- Let them know if there are witnesses to the abuse—this includes your children.

- Tell the police about other violent incidents against you.

- Show them any court documents you have such as a "no contact" or "restraining" order.

- Before signing the police report, read it over carefully. If you find any mistakes, have them corrected.

- Ask the police for information concerning community resources that can help you, such as shelters, hot lines, counseling services, and advocacy.

- Before the police leave, ask for the case number of their report and a phone number to call should you want to follow up on the case. Write down the name, badge number, and precinct name of the officers who came, as well as the date and time they arrived. If you ever need to get a copy of the police report, or to find the officers to have them testify for you in court, you will need this information.

Consider pressing charges. You can wait a day or two to decide if this is the best thing for you to do. It may seem harsh, but again this may be the most loving thing you can do for your husband because it will make him realize he cannot continue his abusiveness and get away with it. The court can order him to have no contact with you for the duration of his sentence. This may motivate him to go for counseling, in fact they can order him to get counseling or alcoholic treatment.

Once you decide to press charges, it's important to follow through. Your husband must see that you are ready to assume the responsibility of taking care of yourself. He must recognize your insistence that things cannot go on the way they are.

Reconciling with your husband before he's brought to court will probably cause you to feel a lot of pressure to drop the charges. If you live in a state where only the prosecutor or the judge can dismiss those charges, it will make things easier. You can honestly say that the matter is out of your hands.

Determine whether you should file a court action. Should you decide to do so, do it as soon as possible after the attack. The longer you wait, the less serious people will think you are about stopping the battering. The memories of the witnesses will fade, your injuries will heal and your resolve will weaken.

Should you go to court, you cannot simply ask for help. The law doesn't allow you to do that. You must make specific requests. Do you want a restraining order? If you aren't sure, see a lawyer who can explain the various possibilities available from the courts in your state.

As a Christian, you may be hesitant to involve the authorities in your domestic problems. You may feel that it is something you must work out for yourself. But please remember: The purpose of the law is to protect you. It does have its weaknesses; still, it can offer you help and protection—but only if you use it!

But your own protection is only part of the picture. By making your husband see the cost of his actions, and by forcing him to pay the price for them, you may help to bring around his reform. By beating you he is committing a crime, just as surely as if he were committing a robbery or dealing in drugs. Being arrested and having to deal with the law may actually help him to gain a proper perspective on his crime.

Being submissive to the laws of the land means living within the framework of our civil laws and abiding by the authority of our government as long as its laws do not conflict with the law of God.

1. "Wife Beating: The Silent Crime," *Time* (September 5, 1983), p.23.
2. Ibid.

9

INDIVIDUAL
HELPING AND HEALING

"Something's wrong, Jim," Marilyn told her husband one Saturday afternoon. "Something's wrong, and I should be doing something about it, but I don't know what to do."

Although anxious to get the dresser ready for its first coat of stain, Jim put down the sandpaper and looked up at his wife. All day he had been aware something was bothering her. "What's up?" he asked.

"I don't know exactly," she explained hesitantly. "Let me tell you what happened, then tell me what you think. Do you remember Janet, the woman who has been in my Bible study group off and on for the past year and a half? Well, she's back, and I've made a real effort to befriend her.

"Yesterday I noticed bruises on her arms and neck. Without thinking, I commented that she must be like me—easily bruised. She seemed terribly embarrassed at my comment and made some excuse about how clumsy she was, always bumping into things and falling."

"That does sound like you," Jim laughed.

"I don't know," Marilyn continued. "There's more to it than just the bruises. Janet seems so nervous, so insecure, so . . . well, so afraid. Once when we were discussing the Christian husband's position as head of the home, she sat and cried through the entire session. Something's wrong, Jim, I just know it."

Jim stared at his wife. "What are you trying to say, Marilyn?" he said evenly. "I know Roger—not well, but well enough. If you are suggesting that he is to blame for Janet's bruises and fear . . ." He didn't finish his statement. It all seemed too incredible.

"What should I do?" Marilyn asked quietly.

"Why not talk to Janet?"

"Oh, I couldn't do that!" Marilyn exclaimed. "What would I say? What if I'm wrong?"

"What if you're right?" Jim replied.

After a time of prayer together with her husband, Marilyn called Janet and invited her over for coffee Monday morning. To her surprise, Janet replied that Roger was out at the park with the children and wasn't due back for several hours. Since Janet was free, Marilyn asked, would it be convenient for her to come right away?

Sitting together over coffee, the two women chatted about children, church, and their Bible study group. Suddenly Marilyn reached over and took her friend's hand.

"Janet," she said earnestly, "I have the feeling that something is wrong. Please don't think that I'm butting into your business, but I am really concerned. Do you want to talk?"

That's all she needed to say. As Marilyn listened in shocked silence, Janet poured out her desperate story. When her words were gone, her tears began—tears of despair, tears of loneliness, tears of humiliation, tears for all her shattered dreams.

Together they prayed, two friends seeking God's wisdom and guidance in the handling of a shared problem.

As she turned to go, Janet thanked Marilyn for calling. "I needed someone badly," she said. "Someone who would listen and believe me, someone who would help me sort out my feelings. I needed you, Marilyn."

THE NEED FOR HELP AND SUPPORT

Marilyn knew very little about wife battering, and even less about counseling. Yet she cared enough about a hurting sister to reach out to her, even though it meant risking embarrassment and possible rejection.

Many battered women are experts at hiding their problems. They wear makeup and long-sleeved clothes that cover their bruises and injuries. When they can't cover them, they invent logical stories to explain them away. And yet there are subtle things that may arouse suspicion: A woman who wears sunglasses inside or when the sun isn't shining, one who is constantly making excuses for injuries, or one who seems afraid of her husband or whose children seem afraid of their father.

Like Janet, most abused women find it very difficult to ask for help. It's humiliating to let people know that your husband is using you as a punching bag. And it's easy to assume no one really cares. Concerned family and friends can help a battered woman be open to their care and support by making it clear that they are concerned, and that they are willing to listen whenever she wants to talk. They can point out articles on wife abuse, or bring up the subject in a general way, then discuss the help available to battering victims. In addition, every concerned person should be very careful never to become involved in jokes or comments that would lend an air of acceptance to the abuser's behavior.

Afraid that his wife will leave him if she knows anyone who will help her, many an abusive husband will try hard to keep his wife isolated. A compassionate friend can be the best—perhaps the only—helper a battered woman has.

But before a person reaches out to a victim or an abuser, she must be sure that she can actually follow through with her ministry of loving support—despite the victim's exasperating helplessness and chronic habit of giving her violent husband one more chance. Tough love is just that—tough. It is not easy to be involved in confrontation, support, and restoration. But then, Christ doesn't call us to a life of self-centered comfort.

How Can I Help?

A person who wants to help should clearly understand that wife beating is a serious situation, one that cannot be remedied easily. If you have a friend, relative, or neighbor who is being battered, you can help by doing the following.

If someone tells you she is being abused, believe her. Perhaps her husband doesn't seem the type to do such a thing. Because such violence is so opposed to Christ's commands, it's very difficult to believe such things actually occur in a family that sits every Sunday in the pew in front of us. But if we don't believe it when we are confronted with it, the hard reality of this sin will continue. It's time for Christians to reach out so these families do not have to suffer in silence.

If she is in immediate danger, offer to take her and her children in for a night or two. You can help her find more permanent quarters later.

If you witness a beating, call the police. Don't try to get between the woman and her husband. It is much too dangerous.

Offer her a listening ear and understanding. You may be providing the first or the only opportunity she has to tell her story. Even if she doesn't actually do anything about it, just sharing her situation will help her handle the fear, confusion, and loneliness that are crippling her. Be willing to listen, to believe, to share the woman's questions and struggles. You need say no more than "I care about you. I can see you're in trouble, and I'm willing to do anything I can to help." Don't be judgmental, nor should you try to downplay the trauma of the situation. Battered women need support. People who offer nothing but sweet words of advice and easy solutions are in effect denying the depth of the woman's pain and despair.

Help the battered woman understand that she does indeed have choices. She should find out about local support groups, shelters, and any other available resources. Battered women have options. Help your friend to understand what they are.

A wise helper will also understand there is a limit to what she can do. Because of the complexity of the psychological and emotional damage—not to mention the physical—it is wise counsel to encourage battered women to seek professional help.

Insist that she make her own choices. You may be certain you know what she should do, but your job is to support and to guide, not to take over. Help your friend think through her situation, and encourage her to make decisions that will allow her to improve it. You can help her by sitting down and discussing what needs to take place before she will return to her husband. You can also help her work through the consequences of her decision to leave—financial, emotional, etc. But it is her responsibility to take action. Remember, helplessness and passivity are a great part of her problem.

Individual Helping and Healing

Help her realize that she is not responsible for her husband's violent behavior. It is easy to believe your friend must have done something to incite such violence. To some extent it may be partially her fault. She may need your help or the help of a professional to gain an accurate perception of areas in which she may need to change. However, unless she realizes that her husband's violence is wrong, she may not only stay in a dangerous situation, she will also be much less likely to demonstrate her love for her husband by confronting him with his need to change.

Remind her that God doesn't want her to suffer abuse. She may have learned to accept her situation, to reason that she somehow deserves it or is a better person because of it. That's not true. God loves her, and it is his design that she live without violence in a marriage relationship. God wants her to be treated with love and respect. You may want to discuss with her God's picture of marriage. These discussions could revolve around studies in 1 Corinthians 7 and Ephesians 5:22-33.

Help her to see herself as capable and lovable. That's how God sees her. Point out Scripture verses that demonstrate God's love for each of us.

> For God so loved the world that he gave his one and only Son, that whoever believes in him shall not perish but have eternal life. (John 3:16)

> But God demonstrates his own love for us in this: While we were still sinners, Christ died for us. (Romans 5:8)

> What, then, shall we say in response to this? If God is for us, who can be against us? He who did not spare his own Son, but gave him up for us all—how will he not also, along with him, graciously give us all things? Who will bring any charge against those whom God has chosen? It is God who justifies. Who is he that condemns? Christ Jesus, who died—more than that, who was raised to life—is at the right hand of God and is also interceding for us. Who shall separate us from the love of Christ? Shall trouble or hardship or persecution or famine or nakedness or danger or sword? As it is written:

> "For your sake, we face death all day long;
> we are considered as sheep to be slaughtered."
>
> No, in all these things we are more than conquerors through him who loved us. For I am convinced that neither death nor life, neither angels nor demons, neither the present nor the future, nor any powers, neither height nor depth, nor anything else in all creation, will be able to separate us from the love of God that is in us in Christ Jesus our Lord. (Romans 8:31-39)
>
> How great is the love the Father has lavished on us, that we should be called children of God! And that is what we are! (1 John 3:1)
>
> This is love: not that we loved God, but that he loved us and sent his Son as an atoning sacrifice for our sins. (1 John 4:10)

Be especially careful about urging your battered friend to stay with her husband. Unless he gives evidence that he has changed, assume that the abuse will continue. Confession and contrition are not equivalent to a changed life. By encouraging separation you are not encouraging divorce. By encouraging her to stay you are in effect sanctioning her husband's abusive behavior.

Help her find a support community. Direct other friends, church members, or relatives toward the hurting woman. If she has come to you in confidence, you can do this without going into detail about her situation. Perhaps you might say something like, "Mary especially needs your love and prayers just now. Remember her." You may also want to carefully pray about approaching your church to open up a shelter or have a support group for battered and abused women.

If possible, introduce your friend to other women who have been battered. Sharing with them will encourage and comfort her, and by showing that change is possible, it will allow her to move forward. Unfortunately, there are very few Christian support groups. What the community has to offer is very often feminist in thinking—there is a tremendous void here that only the church and Christ can fill!

Resist the temptation to try to reason with her husband. This probably sounds unchristian, unbiblical; and yet the facts speak for themselves. It almost never works. Until he seeks to change and is willing to receive help, talking will not stimulate behavioral change. The causes of his behavior are usually too ingrained, too complex, for an untrained person to be of any real help.

Be available. Spouse abuse is a complicated problem for both the abused and abuser. Any real solution will take time. Offer your help in specific ways. If the woman needs to make a court appearance, get medical attention, or tend to other business related to the attack, offer to accompany her. While she looks for more permanent housing, goes job hunting or goes for counseling, go with her or offer to watch her children. Encourage her to get out and be with people, invite her to lunch, go to a movie together. Let her know you enjoy her company. Be sensitive: Be available when she needs you, back off when she needs to be alone. Above all, let her know she can count on your friendship, support, and help.

Help her children. Some abused women become so emotionally drained that they are unable to meet their children's needs. You can be a helpful, caring, loving friend with whom her children are welcome to share at any time.

With the permission of their mother, include the children in your family outings. Invite them to spend the night now and then, perhaps an occasional weekend, at your home. Plan such times carefully, being sensitive to their mother's feelings. You must take care not to make her feel that she is doing an inadequate job of mothering. What you do want to do is establish yourself as a stable, loving, dependable person in their lives.

An abused woman has a long, hard road ahead. And while she struggles toward healing, she will be at the mercy of emotions she cannot understand: low self-esteem, guilt, intense loneliness, and deep despair. These women need to be surrounded by people who can encourage, exhort, and support her along her arduous journey. Will you help?

10

WHAT THE CHURCH CAN DO

The more Marilyn thought about Janet, the more helpless she felt. There was only so much she could do for her friend.

Marilyn knew something about helplessness. Less than a year before, after back surgery, she spent six weeks flat in bed. But she wasn't alone. Not only was her husband Jim there to encourage and comfort her, but her church family was there too. Night after night, week after week, they brought over hot dinners for her family. They made sure her children were cared for, her house was clean, and her shopping done. They came to visit, kept her informed of the goings-on of the community, read to her, encouraged and cheered her. Many times during those six weeks, and many times afterward, Marilyn wondered how she could ever have made it without that support.

That's what gave Marilyn the idea. Those same caring Christian brothers and sisters knew Janet. If they were aware of her need for help, surely they would rally around her, too. It wasn't necessary to tell the specifics. It would be enough to let them know that Janet was having problems at home and needed their support. If Janet wanted them to know more, she could tell them.

In our country, with the extended family pretty much a thing of the past, women like Janet are often left to their own devices. When the pressures and stresses of life get too great, they find little help and support available.

That's where the church can come in. As the family of God, we are called to a ministry of love and healing. We can do it individually, we can do it as families, we can do it as church leaders, and we can do it as a Christian community.

In an article in the *Southwest Baptist Conference Social Ministries Quarterly*, Ardi Erickson describes what happened when she asked God to show her how to respond to a brother or sister in need.[1] A happy woman, she lived with her pastor husband and two daughters in a lovely suburban home, enjoying her parttime nursing job. Since childhood she had experienced a secure relationship with the Lord.

Then in January of 1974 she came across two verses that were to change her life: "But whoever has the world's goods, and beholds his brother in need and closes his heart against him, how does the love of God abide in him? Little children, let us not love with word or with tongue, but in deed and truth" (1 John 3:17-18 NASB).

Mrs. Erickson relates how she meditated upon this passage, asking the Lord to show her how it applied to her. He did. Before long three children, left homeless when their mother was murdered by their father, became part of the Erickson family. Determined to do something about the type of violence that had claimed the life of the children's mother, Ardi, her husband Bruce, and several other couples at Covenant Baptist Church of Columbus, Ohio, established Heidi House, the first long-term Christian shelter for battered women in the United States. Says Mrs. Erickson, "During the years that followed, hundreds of women and children experienced God's love, peace, and healing in their lives."[2]

GUIDANCE FROM THE CLERGY

Often the challenge to reach out to others presents itself in the form of a crisis. In a survey conducted among several thousand pastors from conservative Protestant churches, eighty-four percent said that they had counseled at least one woman who had been physically abused by her husband. Thirty-six percent of those had counseled more than six.[3]

How did the ministers in this survey fare as counselors? Well, it depends on whom you ask. James Alsdurf reports that seventy percent of the Christian women with whom he spoke reported that their ministers had minimized the impact of the violence they experienced. The ministers had a different opinion. In his evaluation of the survey Alsdurf concludes, "The pastors in our study tend to overestimate their preparedness as counselors to effectively deal with the abuse."[4]

Granted, counseling abused women and abusive men can be difficult, frustrating, and emotionally draining. In addition to the social and legal implications, there are religious issues which need to be addressed. Questions about separation and divorce, family authority, Christian responsibility, the meaning of suffering, and the possibility of forgiveness are all critical concerns to those touched by family violence. None of these issues have easy answers.

Alsdurf comments that pastors who responded to his survey commonly expressed "uncertainty about how to lovingly respond to an abused woman while at the same time remaining faithful to largely literalistic interpretations of biblical passages on marriage, divorce, and the role of women."[5] In order to be prepared to deal effectively, ministers would do well to prayerfully consider these issues ahead of time. Under what circumstances are they prepared to recommend that an abused woman separate from her husband? How about divorce? How will they explain the biblical principles of submission?

Misconceptions about biblical passages are partly to blame for the actions of abusive husbands, especially within the Christian community. Certainly we have a responsibility to present what the Scripture says without attempting to adjust it to what we want it to say. But before we speak out dogmatically, we must be very sure we correctly understand the Scriptures. There is no biblical basis for abusive behavior. Wife abuse is a sin, one the church must be willing to confront.

The church needs to bring balance and accuracy into its teachings on marriage and submission. Troubled couples must come to see that marriage should be a partnership in which the man is commanded to love his wife. Each is to build the other up, and together they are to recognize Christ as the ultimate head of their home.

With a strong voice, the church must challenge the idea that family violence is a private matter, an area out-of-bounds to anyone outside the family. Unless we speak out, how can we have an impact on the shaping of public opinion? The church needs to take a definite theological stand on marital violence.

It is unlikely, however, that a local congregation will choose to address domestic violence unless the minister leads the way. It is he who must take the initiative.

A minister can begin by accepting the fact that no congregation—including his own—is immune to domestic violence.

Marie Fortune, director of the Center for the Prevention of Sexual and Domestic Violence in Seattle, relates that during the final session of a several-weeks-long seminar for the clergy, one pastor told of encountering two incest cases and a rape in his small congregation. By announcing from the pulpit that he was taking the seminar on sexual and domestic violence, and that he thought the course to be valuable, he apparently gave the congregation "permission" to bring these problems to him with the confidence that he would be able to help.[6]

Not only did that minister let the congregation know that he was interested, but he prepared himself to respond in a sensitive and helpful way by obtaining special training. Without such training, however well-intentioned a minister might be, a misunderstanding of the problem can end up causing even further damage to an already shattering situation.

No one expects a minister to be an expert on every issue that might possibly surface within his congregation. It isn't possible. But he can familiarize himself with other resources in the community and be ready to refer the troubled person to the appropriate sources of help. (See Resources in Appendix 1.)

THE CHURCH CAN HELP

It was a special issue of the Fuller Theological Seminary alumni magazine that first made the ministers at Burnaby Christian Fellowship in Vancouver, British Columbia, acutely aware of the scope of wife abuse. They knew they had to do something. According to Patrick Ducklow, one of the pastors at the church, couples entangled in domestic violence quickly became a part of their extensive counseling ministry.

At Burnaby Christian Fellowship, couples are counseled together. "Of course we work toward reconciliation," says Rev. Ducklow. "But our first goal is conciliation. It is vital that both partners understand what is happening. Before they can be helped, they must gain insight into how they got where they are."

Burnaby Christian Fellowship is not alone in aggressively working with violent families. Other congregations, especially larger ones, are beginning to address the problem. Even some denominations are taking a definite stand. The United Methodist Church and The United Church of Christ are two which have done so. The Catholic Church has long been involved in a ministry of loving care and practical assistance to victims of domestic violence as has the Salvation Army. But these are the exceptions. Most are doing nothing.

WHAT CAN BE DONE?

What about churches which do not have the official support and assistance of their denominations? What about those which lack the finances and the manpower to set up an indepth program? What about Christian communities which want to do something, but not necessarily within the confines of a specific congregation? Is there anything these groups can do? Absolutely! All it takes is a few concerned Christians who see the need and are ready to get involved.

Any group can provide practical assistance to victims of abuse. When emotionally distraught mothers need to have their children out of the house for a time, volunteer babysitters can give them the break they need. Women who flee their homes need help in locating housing and finding jobs. Many need financial assistance. All need nonjudgmental support, encouragement, and prayer.

Underlying any active response must be an attitude response. Eva Baranoff, clinical director of S.A.F.E. (Stop Abusive Family Environment), stresses that anyone working with abused women or abusive men must put the responsibility for the violence where it belongs—on the batterer. Even though the victim may be partially responsible for problems in her marriage, perhaps even the argument that set off a beating, she is not responsible for the violence.

Judi Bumstead, Director of Family Ministries at Trinity Baptist Church in Santa Barbara, California, is one who would like to see the Christian community take action. A Licensed Marriage, Family, and Child Counselor, Judi has had the opportunity to work with battered women, and she has specific suggestions for local Christian groups who want to help by counseling these women.

As a first step, Judi suggests forming a core of individuals who really want to make a difference. They need not be professionals, but they do need to be trained. It is dangerous and unfair to ask even the most well-meaning volunteers to work beyond their training and experience.

Resources are available. S.A.F.E., a program run through the psychology department at Fuller Theological Seminary in Pasadena, California, has much to offer concerned Christians. Besides counseling services, referrals and legal advocacy, they can help with the training of counselors. The Center for the Prevention of Sexual and Domestic Violence in Seattle, Washington, is another organization that offers a wide range of services, including a workshop manual for clergy and others who want to help. (See Appendix 1 for more information on this helpful resource.)

For groups without access to such professional Christian organizations, Judi Bumstead suggests looking to a resource that is available almost everywhere—the community shelter for battered women. Because they are generally underfunded and understaffed, most shelters welcome volunteers. In exchange for their services, volunteers will be trained and will have an opportunity to gain experience which could be helpful to the Christian community. (See Appendix 1 for organizations which can provide a listing of the shelters throughout the country.)

Core group members need each other. It is important that they meet together regularly to discuss experiences, to pray together, to share ideas, to support and encourage each other, to together seek the strength, guidance, and wisdom of the Lord.

Once a core group has received training and experience, they will be in a position to expand their ministry. A good start would be to raise awareness. They can sponsor meetings—perhaps featuring a speaker, tapes, or a film on the subject of wife abuse—then close with specific suggestions for involvement. If regular women's ministries meetings are held, one could be devoted to wife abuse. A series on women's concerns might be presented, or one on getting involved in the community. Either could include domestic violence.

On a broader scale, it is important that the Christian community rise up and make its voice heard. We must be advocates of compassion and justice. This may mean speaking out on behalf of individuals who need immediate help or it may mean advocating on a larger scale—to change unfair laws that cause further suffering to the victims and do nothing to bring batterers toward healing, or to spearhead the development of community resources.

SUPPORT GROUPS

When talking about the support group she attended at a community shelter, June, a minister's wife, said, "In my support group I said exactly what I felt and no one hated me for it. I told the others what my husband had done to me, and never once did they tell me it was my fault. I was accepted and understood. Those women knew from first-hand experience what I needed, and they were ready and able to give it to me."

After several minutes June added, "But I also had questions they couldn't answer—questions about submission to my husband, about God and why he let this happen to me. I would really have appreciated a Christian perspective. Why don't churches sponsor groups like that?"

Why indeed? Battered women often suffer a crippling sense of isolation, loneliness, and powerlessness. When they receive support, advice and encouragement from others who have been there, their chances for healing are greatly enhanced. And if the support group includes women who have survived abusive relationships and have gone on to enjoy healthy, happy lives—women who have discovered some answers to their questions about God's love and care for them—those who are just beginning the long road to recovery will see that a brighter tomorrow really is possible. Through them, battering victims can gain the strength and courage to leave the past behind.

Besides understanding and loving encouragement, Christian support groups can offer the added dimension of prayer support and a scriptural understanding of God's loving control in even the most difficult of circumstances.

Because wife abuse is a complex and potentially deadly problem, it is important that support groups either be led by a professional—a social worker, family counselor or psychologist—or else be under the direction or supervision of a trained professional. Members of the core group who have received training may feel confident enough to head up a group, especially if there is a professional upon whom they could call should a problem arise.

Some churches prefer to hire counselors. A congregation can take on the financial support or the group can charge the participants. Whatever the specific arrangements, the support group should be looked upon as a ministry. No one should be turned away simply because she cannot pay.

To establish a support group, all that is needed is a place to meet, a trained leader, and a couple of people willing to be involved in the group. A small beginning is fine. Word will get around. Notify the local Salvation Army chapter, the community women's shelter, Christian counselors, the YMCA and YWCA, and local churches. Make it known that there is a Christian support group available for abused women.

Support group meetings should be upbeat, encouraging, nonjudgmental and nonthreatening. Women should be encouraged to share their experiences, their frustrations, and their questions. Every battered woman needs to know that the problems she faces are not unique to her; others struggle with the same things. Together they can study God's word. Together they can lay their problems before the Lord. Together they can rejoice over victories.

PREVENTION

The best way to deal with family violence is to help prevent it from occurring in the first place. The church's preventive role is, in the long run, the most important of all. By developing an in-depth program of premarital counseling—one that realistically approaches subjects such as anger, conflict and violence— a couple can discuss what each will do should violence ever occur. They should be encouraged to set ground rules with each other in advance and to establish a fair and workable way of dealing with the conflicts that are sure to arise in their marriage.

But family education should not stop with premarital counseling. Parenting classes, marriage enrichment workshops, family communication workshops—all of these are excellent opportunities to help families learn how to shape and develop relationships in nonviolent, supportive, positive ways. By equipping families to develop caring, nurturing, loving relationships, the cycle of violence can be broken.

Shelters—Places of Sanctuary

When a violent man is out of control, the thing his wife needs most is a place of safety for herself and her children. Churches have traditionally been known as places of sanctuary. It can still be so.

Without a doubt there is a real need for more shelters, especially ones that operate from a Christian point of view. The problem is that setting up and maintaining a shelter is a difficult and expensive task, one which few churches have the personnel or the finances to undertake. Still, it is a project the Christian community would do well to evaluate. Information on how to start, fund, staff and operate shelters is available for churches and Christian groups who are interested (see Appendix 1).

Covenant Baptist Church in Columbus responded to the need for shelter by founding Heidi House. Burnaby Christian Fellowship in Vancouver responded in a different way: by establishing transition homes, the homes of Christians who are willing to provide emergency shelter. Judi Bumstead suggests creating a network of homes from different churches in the community, so that women will be able to be sheltered in places their husbands would be unlikely to look.

Although running sheltering homes is not as forbidding a task as establishing a shelter, it is nevertheless an exhausting program. Not everyone has the time, the personality, or the

118

flexibility to have their home used. Rev. Duckworth emphasizes that a very special type of person is needed to provide such a home. "Not rescuers," he insists. Eva Baranoff agrees. She says that such workers need to take a very specific approach—certainly not cold or detached, but at the same time not overly sympathetic. Shelterers need a fine balance of supportiveness and objectivity.

Certainly a screening procedure must be used in the selection of sheltering homes and families. This, as well as the entire program, should be under the supervision of a professional.

Violent men are dangerous men. Some restrict their violence to the privacy of their own homes. Others, if their wives leave, will attack the women wherever they are. Still others will strike out in fury at anyone who dares to get between them and their wives. Because they are dealing with violent men, there are always potential risks to those who shelter abuse victims. Under no circumstances is it appropriate to use a volunteer's home if it is known that the victim's spouse is likely to pose a threat to them. Furthermore, the location of sheltering homes should always be kept secret. If a woman tells her husband where she is—and many will—she should be removed at once.

CAN THE CHURCH HELP THE BATTERER?

When a woman is battered and abused, our main concern is for her. That's as it should be. But as Christians, we must also be concerned about the abuser. He, too, is a recipient of God's love and mercy. Healing is also possible for him. So is forgiveness.

A husband who is allowed to continue his violent behavior is done no favor. Experts agree that battering men rarely seek help unless they are pressured into it. Although they vow over and over that never again will they hurt their wives, every promise is broken. The fact is, they cannot simply will themselves to change. The low overall cure rate for abusers is proof of that.

Pastors or lay counselors may be able to help an abuser by confronting him directly. He must be forced to face the reality of what he is doing to his wife, to his children, and to himself.

Someone needs to care enough to say, "This has got to stop." It is much easier to do this if the wife and children are removed from the home.

Confrontation is not the same as being judgmental. It can and should be supportive. It should encourage the abuser to see that his actions are wrong. It should encourage him to seek treatment. It should also offer him the hope of healing and forgiveness through Jesus Christ. It should offer to be a support to him.

When confronting a batterer, let him know *it is his behavior that's unacceptable, not he himself.* He needs to understand that he is accepted by God, and that God is a loving heavenly Father, not a cruel authoritarian like his earthly father may have been. Through the perfect love of God he can be healed, but this can happen only if he is willing to be obedient to God's mandates.

Christian men who are willing to befriend a batterer and to accept him in the love of Christ can be vital to his healing. Such relationships will give an abuser a chance to talk out some of his feelings and emotions and it will also give him a model of what it means to be a gentle, loving man.

All of this should be in addition to, not instead of, professional counseling. Simply feeling accepted and cared for is not enough. The batterer needs to learn that beating is not the way to release tension and anger. He must understand that battering is not a part of all marriage relationships. The happy, satisfying ones are based on love and consideration for each other.

Couples who develop friendships with battering husbands and their wives also have the unique opportunity of acting as role models, of showing by example that there are constructive ways to release anger and handle marital problems. But this is no easy assignment. It takes great persistence and patience, and it takes a deep reliance on the Lord and much prayer.

One word of warning: Beware of the man who is full of contrite words and promises that are not backed up by actions. Some batterers can be very calculating, not only in how they deal with their wives, but also in how they deal with the authorities and their counselors. With disarming charm, they can play therapy against the court system, and escape ever having to assume responsibility for their deeds. Remember, abusive men are usually convinced that they are doing nothing wrong.

Most batterers remain unhealed because they are not willing to submit themselves to counseling and to persistence in attempting difficult change. But difficult does not mean impossible.

As Christians, we have a responsibility to do everything we can to assist repentant abusive men along the road to recovery. What better testimony is there to the power of God than the healing of someone society has written off as hopeless?

Wife battering hurts. As long as it is kept silent, it will go on hurting, even within the body of Christ. The church has a ministry to perform, but how can we respond to the cry of victims we do not see?

For the abused wife, the church can be a place of refuge and aid while she searches for a way through her maze of confusion. We can help the batterer by confronting him with the reality of what he is doing, and by helping him understand the meaning of marriage as it was ordained by God. To the entire family we can offer support, encouragement, and a working model of a healthy family relationship. Christ's loving compassion compels us to do nothing less.

Yes, there is hope for battered wives, and for battering husbands, too. Only through the healing hands of Christ does complete recovery come. And it is our hands that the Lord uses to reach out and help the hurting.

1. Ardi Erickson, "Battling Violence on the Home Front," *Southwest Baptist Conference Social Ministries Quarterly* (Winter 1986), p.1.

2. Ibid.

3. James and Phyllis Alsdurf, "Wife Abuse and the Church," *Evangelical Newsletter* (January 17, 1986), p.1.

4. Ibid.

5. Ibid.

6. Marie M. Fortune, "The Church and Domestic Violence," *Theology, News and Notes* (Fuller Seminary, June 1982), p.17.

EPILOGUE

Janet was finishing the dinner dishes when Roger called in to her. "Did you pick my shirts up at the laundry?"

"Oh, Honey, I forgot!" Janet replied. "And I was downtown, too! I'm so sorry. I'll do it first thing in the morning."

"First thing in the morning is too late. I need a clean shirt for my meeting tomorrow. You're the laziest person I've ever known!"

"I'm really sorry, Roger," Janet said evenly. "It was careless of me, but anyone can forget. You can't expect me to be perfect."

Slowly, deliberately, Roger laid down the coffee cup he was holding. He walked across the room and positioned himself directly in front of his wife. When he spoke, it was in a low, threatening voice. "You know what I expect of you, Janet. I expect you to be a decent, thoughtful wife. But it's becoming more and more clear to me that for some reason you are determined not to meet my expectations."

With sudden alarm Janet noticed that Roger's fists were clenched so tightly that his knuckles had turned white.

"I really am sorry, Roger," she said quickly. "I'll wash and iron a shirt for you tonight."

"You certainly will," he hissed through clenched teeth. "But the shirt is not the important thing here. The important thing is your attitude. Something has to be done about that."

In terror Janet fled to the bathroom and locked the door.

When Roger called in to her, it was not with a voice of anger, but of reason. "Come on, open the door, Janet. Let's discuss this like adults."

Janet's heart jumped with joyful relief. Roger wasn't going to hit her. He just wanted to talk. Feeling foolish for having run and hidden like a child, she unlocked the door and opened it wide. "I'm sorry. I . . ." But the look on Roger's face caused her to freeze in mid-sentence.

Without a word Roger pushed Janet over to the bathtub which was still full of water from Christy's evening bath. Seized with violent rage, he grabbed her and pushed her head under the water. She fought and kicked, but Roger was stronger. He held her under.

After what seemed an eternity, Roger released his wife. She came up gasping for air. Weak and petrified with fear, coughing and sputtering, she pleaded with him to leave her alone. He would not.

Insane with rage, Roger shoved Janet's face back into the tub. She tried to scream, but succeeded only in choking on a mouthful of water.

And then, as suddenly as it had begun, the attack ended. "There, now," he said calmly. "I hope you have learned your lesson so that we won't have to go through this again."

As Janet lay on the bathroom floor coughing and gasping for air, Roger nonchalantly returned to his coffee and evening newspaper.

The whole thing was beyond understanding. All that insanity, rage and near-death over a shirt at the laundry! It wasn't right. It wasn't normal. It mustn't continue.

By the time she had caught her breath, Janet's head was clear. Her mind was made up. As noiselessly as possible, she went to her bedroom and took the suitcase off the the top shelf of the closet. She packed a few necessities, a change of clothes, the cash she had carefully hidden away, the checkbook, several documents, and the children's baby pictures. Then she took down another suitcase and packed several outfits for each of the children, warm sweaters, and the math book David had brought home so that he could finish his division.

From her bedside table she picked up her new Bible with the burgundy leather cover. Opening the front pages she read this inscription: "To my dearest Janet, whom I will love forever. Your husband, Roger." As she tucked the Bible into the suitcase, her eyes filled with her first tears of the evening. "Oh, Roger," she whispered, "why does it have to end like this?"

Janet tiptoed into her son's room and gently shook the sleeping child. "Get up quickly, David, and don't make a sound."

"What's happening, Mom?" he asked, rubbing his sleepy eyes.

"Never mind. Just do as I say. I'll explain it later."

"Is it Daddy?"

Epilogue

"I'll explain later," Janet said again. "Put on your jacket and shoes, go quietly out the back door and wait in the car. I'll get Christy, and we'll meet you there."

David got up and solemnly did as he was told. His maturity made Janet proud, but it also made her heart ache. He was, after all, only a little boy. Why should he have to know so much about pain and fear and danger and violence?

Janet and her children went to Marilyn's where they were welcomed and made comfortable. After tucking the exhausted little ones into bed, Marilyn made a pot of hot tea. Then she sat and listened as Janet poured out her story of anger and frustration. Marilyn hugged her when the tears came, and asked her no questions.

"Did I do the right thing?" Janet asked. "Was I right to leave him?"

"Your life was in danger," Marilyn replied. "You did what you had to do." Reaching over, she took Janet's hand.

Janet and her children stayed with Marilyn for almost a week, long enough for her to make some serious decisions. She determined that no longer would she subject herself or her children to Roger's uncontrollable rage. She would not go back to him without evidence of repentance. Together they would make a written agreement of the rules of their home—in particular her right to be safe from violence and a commitment from him that he was ready and willing to change his behavior. He would have to prove that commitment by getting treatment from a qualified counselor, and he must stay with it long enough for her to see that he was committed to it—six months, she decided.

Since Roger didn't know Marilyn, it took him several days to trace Janet's whereabouts. When he finally located her, he called and pleaded with her to come back home. But by then Janet had gained enough self-confidence to give him her ultimatum: "I will no longer put up with being hit." Before she could tell him the rest of her conditions, he hung up.

At the end of the week Janet moved into an apartment nearby. Accompanied by Marilyn and her husband, Janet returned to her house to collect her and the children's belongings. Though Roger knew they were coming, he chose not to be home.

On moving day, a man from the church came to help Jim move Janet in. David and Christy spent the day playing at the home of a woman in Janet and Marilyn's Bible study group.

All day Marilyn and Janet cleaned cupboards, lined drawers, and unpacked boxes. At five o'clock, the doorbell rang. It was Ruth and Kathy, two women from church that Janet hardly knew.

"We brought you lasagna and strawberry pie," Ruth said with a smile.

"Why?" Janet asked. "Why would you do this for me?"

"Marilyn told us you two would be working all day," Kathy answered. "We figured you'd be too tired to fix dinner."

"I know I would!" said Ruth.

The supportive friendships from her church friends didn't stop when Janet was settled into her new apartment. Through thoughtful gestures, phone calls, and visits, they let her know that she was important to them and that they were concerned about her.

While Janet and her children were surrounded by loving concern, Roger sat at home wondering what had gone wrong. Hadn't he accepted his position as head of his family, just as he had been taught to do? Hadn't he loved and disciplined them? Hadn't he done his best to make them a good home? Okay, so he had gone overboard with Janet; he admitted that. But everyone makes mistakes; that was no reason for her to take the kids and leave. Nothing could justify that.

When he received a call from Jim, who suggested they meet for lunch, Roger was suspicious. It could be some kind of a trap. Still, he was anxious to find out how Janet and the kids were doing, so in the end he accepted the invitation.

"I'm concerned about you, Roger," Jim told him at lunch. "What you did to Janet was wrong. You need help."

Epilogue

Roger bristled and immediately grew defensive. He informed Jim that he had no business interfering in his life. In no uncertain terms Roger insisted that his relationship with Janet was between himself and God and no one else. Then he accused Jim of influencing Janet to leave him.

Gently but firmly Jim told Roger what Janet had related to Marilyn. "This time she's not coming back, Roger," he said. "Not until things change. It's up to you."

The next day Roger received a call from the pastor. To his amazement, the man was suggesting an appointment with a counselor. "He specializes in problems like yours, Roger," the minister said.

Furious, Roger hung up on him. Who did that man think he was? It was Janet who had the problem, not him!

As time went on, Janet had a great deal of time to remember and consider. At last she was free to be herself. No more did she need to scrutinize Roger in an effort to keep track of his shifting moods. No more did she need to constantly be on her guard in order to ward off his sudden attacks of violence. And yet she was lonely, so very lonely.

Janet had always believed that marriage is for keeps. Even though Roger's brutality had splintered their vows to love, honor, respect and cherish, she didn't want to call it quits. As far as she was concerned, this apartment was just someplace where she could be safe while Roger realized his action and attitudes were sin and completely out of line with biblical guidelines. She wanted them to get back together, but she had come to realize that unless Roger realized he had been wrong and unless he sought to change, he would continue to abuse her.

She also knew that though there were no promises, it was possible for her relationship to be repaired. God is a God of redemption and healing. Isn't that what Christianity is all about? Roger could be healed. She could be healed. Her life could return to normal.

And all the time, Jim refused to give up on Roger. "What he did was horrible," he told Marilyn. "But he is not a horrible person."

128

Jim met Roger several times a week—usually for lunch, sometimes for bowling or a church activity. Sometimes they didn't mention Janet and the children at all. But whenever they did talk about the family, Jim stood firm. "You're a nice guy, Roger, but you need help."

And when Roger was alone, he thought—he thought about Janet, he thought about the kids he loved so much, he thought about his dreams of being the head of a happy family. He had been so sure he was right. Yet Jim was just as sure he was wrong. So was the minister. And he couldn't argue that the families he had begun to closely observe were different than his. Maybe, just maybe, he wasn't as right as he had thought.

A long, rough road lies ahead for Janet. The years of abuse cannot be erased overnight, nor even in weeks or months or years. No one should expect that. Whatever happens, scars will remain.

Yet the end to Janet's story is one of hope, one of promise. And why not? God is real. He is all powerful. He is faithful. And he holds those who suffer close to his heart.

APPENDIX I
RESOURCES

Because wife abuse is so widespread, shelters, hotlines, legal aid and counseling groups that deal specifically with this problem have sprung up all over the United States. The purpose of this section is to assist you in finding the help you need.

Whether you are involved in an abusive relationship yourself, or you want to help an abused friend, the following resource suggestions are for you.

For immediate local help:

- Look in the telephone directory under "Mental Health," "Crisis," "Battered Women" or "Help." Most cities, and many smaller communities as well, have specific "hotlines" for battered women.

- Call the police, tell them your situation and ask to be referred to an appropriate community agency. They will have a list of the local resources.

- Call your local Salvation Army unit. Many have emergency shelter facilities and information.

Further information on the subject of wife abuse is available from the following:

Center for Women Policy Studies
2000 P Street, N.W. Suite 508
Washington, D.C. 20036
(202) 872-1770

This center is funded by the Law Enforcement Assistance Administration in order to provide technical assistance to anyone involved in domestic violence. It keeps a constantly updated resource file in its office where people can locate the resources closest to their homes.

National Coalition against Domestic Violence
1500 Massachusetts Avenue, N.W. #35
Washington, D.C. 20005

This group can provide additional information on local shelters and hotlines.

Women Against Violence Emergency Services
(WAVES)
P.O. Box 1121
Berkeley, California 94701 (415) 527-HELP

WAVES makes referrals to local shelters throughout the country. The following resources are especially for those who want to be in a position to help battered women:

Center for the Prevention of Sexual
and Domestic Violence
1914 North 34th Street, Suite 205
Seattle, WA 98103
(206) 634-1903

An interreligious educational organization, this center can be a helpful resource for the religious community. It provides clergy and lay counselors, as well as secular professionals, with help in the area of family violence. Among other services, it provides education and workshops for church workers to teach them how to deal with the problem locally. They have prepared a workshop manual which can be purchased from the center for $10.00.

As a further resource to the religious community, the center also puts out a bimonthly newsletter entitled "Working Together." It can be ordered at the above address.

There are not many organizations whose specific purpose is to help abusive men. If he is fortunate, a man who wants to change will be able to locate one of the following organizations in his community:

Batterers Anonymous
P.O. Box 29
Redlands, California 92373
(714) 383-3643

The Batterers Anonymous program is based on the Alcoholics Anonymous model. Many organizations concerned with domestic violence have established chapters as part of their services. To see if there is one in your area, contact local women's shelters and social service agencies, and check the telephone book under "Batterers Anonymous."

Any group interested in starting a Batterers Anonymous group can order the B.A. program manual from the above address. The cost is $7.00.

Appendix 1: Resources

Emerge
25 Huntington Avenue
Boston, Massachusetts 02116
(617) 267-7690

Emerge is a counseling service for abusive men. Both information and materials are available from them. Besides counseling and treatment, they offer a range of workshops and educational classes.

APPENDIX II
BOOKS, PAMPHLETS
AND TAPES

Baly, Jeanne, "Domestic Violence," a taped workshop available for $4.00 prepaid from:

> Evangelical Women's Caucus
> Box 55
> Newtonville, Massachusetts 02160

Davidson, Terry, *Conjugal Crime* (New York: Hawthorne Books, 1978).

The daughter of a minister who grew up watching her father batter her mother, the author writes vividly of the many emotions of the battered woman. This is a secular book.

Dobson, James, *Love Must Be Tough* (Waco, Texas: Word Books, 1983).

While this book does not deal exclusively with battered women, it does offer practical advice to those who are trapped in difficult family situations. Dr. Dobson writes from a Christian perspective. Besides a section specifically dealing with battering, he also addresses the questions of submission, divorce and forgiveness.

Family Violence: A Workshop Manual for Clergy and Other Service Providers available from:

> National Clearinghouse on Domestic Violence
> P.O. Box 2309
> Rockville, Maryland 20852

A very complete manual, this contains suggested workshops of various lengths, detailed information about conducting the workshops and readings concerning the topics. The cost is $5.00.

Fortune, Marie, and Hormann, Denise, *Family Violence: A Workshop Manual for Clergy and Other Service Providers* (Seattle: Center for the Prevention of Sexual and Domestic Violence, 1980).

Green, Holly Wagner, *Turning Fear to Hope* (Nashville: Thomas Nelson Publishers, 1984).

This book deals with the problem of abuse from a Christian perspective. It includes a discussion of those areas usually ignored in secular resources—submission, divorce, forgiveness.

Lovett, C.S., *The Compassionate Side of Divorce* (Baldwin Park, California: Personal Christianity, 1978).

In dealing with divorce from a biblical viewpoint, the author offers hope and healing for the Christian faced with a broken relationship.

Martin, Del, *Battered Wives* (San Francisco: Glide Publication, 1976).

This book, written from a secular point of view, was one of the first on the subject of wife abuse. It contains a solid overview of the problem, and includes a detailed listing and description of shelters.

Massachusetts Coalition of Battered Women Service Groups, *For Shelter and Beyond: An Educational Manual for Working with Women Who Are Battered* (1981).

To order send $5.00 to:

> Massachusetts Coalition of Battered
> Women Service Groups
> 355 Boylston Street, 4th Floor
> Boston, MA 02116

This is an excellent resource for training volunteers and staff of shelters and other service groups. This manual provides an excellent introduction to many of the issues and conflicts that arise in groups serving battered women.

Plain Talk about Wife Abuse is a free government booklet available from:

> Superintendent of Documents
> Consumer Information Center
> Pueblo, CO 81009

Stolz, B.A., *Violence in the Family: A National Concern, A Church Concern* (Washington D.C.: Office of Domestic Social Development, U.S. Catholic Conference).

A general discussion of domestic violence is presented, and activities that church groups can undertake to respond to the problems recommended. Examples of successful programs are provided to illustrate the type of services that churches can support. These include crisis nurseries and shelters for the abused.

Strom, Kay Marshall, *Helping Women in Crisis* (Grand Rapids: Zondervan, 1986).

Designed to assist ministers, women's ministries workers, and other nonprofessionals in various facets of crisis counseling, this book has a chapter dealing with meeting the needs of abused women and their husbands. Includes a section of do's and don'ts of counseling and a comprehensive resource section.

Walker, Lenore, *The Battered Woman* (New York: Harper & Row, 1979).

In this book, also secular, the author presents a clear and thorough picture of wife abuse. She discusses the problem of "learned helplessness," the paralyzing state in which many abused wives find themselves.

Warrior, Betsy, *Battered Women's Directory*.

Available from the author at 46 Pleasant Street, Cambridge, MA 02139, this 275-page publication is probably the most comprehensive listing of the programs dealing with battered women. It provides a state-by-state listing of shelters and services for battered women, not only in this country but in over thirty other countries as well. It also contains a great deal of practical information on how to set up and operate services for abused women. The cost for the directory is $9.50.

The following books, while not specifically on the subject of wife abuse, deal with a closely related subject—the problem of pain. They can be very helpful to a woman who is struggling to understand and answer the question "Why me?" Books on the subject of forgiveness are also included.

Appendix 2: Books, Pamphlets, and Tapes

Augsburger, David, *The Freedom of Forgiveness* (Chicago: Moody, 1973).

Davis, Creath, *Lord, If I Ever Needed You, It's Now* (Palm Springs, California: Ronald N. Haynes Publishers, Inc.).

Donnelly, Doris, *Learning To Forgive* (Nashville: Abingdon, 1982).

Falwell, Jerry, *When It Hurts Too Much to Cry* (Wheaton: Tyndale House Publishers, 1984).

Lewis, C.S., *The Problem of Pain* (New York: MacMillan Co., 1962).

Powell, Paul W., *Why Me, Lord?* (Wheaton, Illinois: Victor Books, 1981).

Smedes, Lewis B, *Forgive and Forget* (San Francisco: Harper and Row, 1984).

Swindoll, Charles, *Recovery* (Waco, Texas: Word Books, 1985).

Vaughn, Ruth, *When God Doesn't Answer, Has He Forsaken Us?* (Grand Rapids: Zondervan).

Wiersbe, Warren, *Why Us? When Bad Things Happen to God's People* (Old Tappan, New Jersey: Fleming H. Revell, 1983).

Yancey, Phillip. *Where Is God When It Hurts?* (Grand Rapids: Zondervan).